FOREVER BUSTER

FOREVER BUSTER

The Films of Buster Keaton

Steve Lambley

ISBN: 978-94-91868-05-4
©2020 Steve Lambley

SLIDE Books, London / The Hague
Typeset by Steve Lambley Information Design

10 9 8 7 6

Contents

Contents

THE THREE KEATONS

Joe, Myra and Buster, have become recognized two a day attractions, in their comedy act which has been playing the circuits with ever increasing success. Joe is the man with the table and Buster, who is a child comedian and not a midget, as miniature edition of his father in the act, can easily be classed with the best. The trio together present one of the strongest acts in vaudeville. They have lately made a tour of the Keith Circuit and the only trouble Mr. Keaton has is the selection of dates from the numerous offers tendered him.

Introduction

Note

The films in which Buster appears in a leading role are listed chronologically, and those in which he has a featured or a cameo role are given at the end of the book, along with his key television appearances.

For convenience, the films are divided into seven categories:

- The Arbuckle–Keaton Shorts
- The Keaton Shorts
- The Keaton Features
- The MGM Years
- The Educational Pictures Shorts
- The Columbia Shorts
- The Independent Years

Of course nothing is ever that simple, and there will be anomalies within these broad divisions – for instance, his first feature, *The Saphead*, was made soon after he started making his own two-reelers and so appears under The Keaton Shorts. He also travelled abroad to make a couple of feature-length films in the middle of his run of Educational Films shorts. But on the whole, the categorisation works and allows a good oversight of Buster's film career.

A word about release dates

The release dates given, which refer to release in the United States (with the exception of *Le Roi des Champs-Élysées* and *Un Duel à Mort*, which didn't get a US release), are specific if the date can be established beyond reasonable doubt. However, for some of the early shorts in particular it's not possible to give an exact date as even sources from the time – press releases, trade paper announcements, etc. – sometimes don't agree. Current reference books and even the American Film Institute database of feature films are not infallible, and on occasion the date of copyright of a film, usually but not always earlier than the release date, has been confused with the date of release. Also, most of his later industrial films were not commercially released as such.

Therefore, where there is doubt over the exact date of release, only the month or year are given.

And about timings

The running times given for the silent shorts are based on the length of what we might call the official currently available version on DVD or Blu-ray. Establishing exact timings of the original films is nigh-on impossible. For the silent films in particular, a number of versions currently exist for various reasons.

Two versions were often shot at the time – one for a domestic audience and one for overseas distribution. Also, films could be re-edited or even re-shot as a result of feedback from preview showings, meaning a number of variants of the same title could be in circulation. And of course over the years, elements of a film may have become lost, or parts taken from different sources and different versions when being reconstructed by archivists. A notable case of this is *The Blacksmith* (p. 64), the bewildering array of versions of which had baffled many, until a recent bit of brilliant detective work by John Bengtson clarified the situation.

As a result, it's very difficult to state the running time of the early films with any degree of certainty, which is why we have opted for the compromise of using the most common versions currently available commercially to act as more of a comparative guide than a definitive reference.

It's also worth bearing in mind that moving pictures originally tended to be measured in terms of feet rather than minutes, and understandably the running time would be rather dependent on the equipment used. A reel would normally be something under 1,000 feet long, and would typically run for a little over 11 minutes. The running time of the current versions of *The Camera-man* give a good illustration of the variability of timings. The 2020 Criterion Blu-ray release runs to 68 minutes, which is more or less the same length as is generally given in reviews of the film at the time of release, whereas the Turner Classic Movies Archive series DVD release from 2004, which has the same content, evidently runs a little more slowly and so lasts 75 minutes.

I n the 1920s, the heyday of silent film, three comic actors reigned supreme. Charlie Chaplin of course, who is still instantly recognisable and still much admired. Harold Lloyd, who is all but forgotten by most movie-goers, despite having once been the epitome of youth and vigour and boy-next-door charm. And Buster Keaton, a supreme artist and technician, an incredibly gifted physical actor and a dedicated film-maker, who evokes more than admiration and radiates more than charm, and indeed inspires genuine love.

And so abideth Chaplin, Lloyd and Keaton, these three; but the greatest of these is Keaton.

Buster's inherent integrity, truthfulness and enthusiasm defined him, both on screen and off. In all that he did, he would search for a truth that made even the most improbable situation credible. And his basic honesty and decency shone through both as an actor and as a man. The essence of his screen persona was, as he himself put it, "a working man and honest". His performances are (largely) unsentimental, his approach (largely) practical, and so what his character achieves is (largely) merited. He lived in the moment and was clearly not a man for nostalgia or regrets. Having given his all, at whatever personal cost, he would move on to the next challenge with barely a backward glance.

For his audience, his gift was his ability to fully engage in any situation, however absurd. Even in his weaker sound films of the 1930s, and even when the effects of his alcoholism were leaving their mark, his character would always be entirely believable. In times of personal adversity, his commitment was always total. And this is equally evident when playing opposite human or non-human co-stars. That he was an animal lover is clear from his work with Roscoe's dog Luke in several of the Arbuckle shorts, with the cow Brown Eyes in *Go West*, the monkey Josephine in *The Cameraman* … He would have a bond with who or whatever he was doing a scene with that was utterly endearing – inhabiting his own character and understanding his on-screen partner to the extent that the connection is palpable. Nothing, however absurd, would be dismissed, but taken at face value and examined in earnest until fully understood.

Taking another arbitrary aspect, it's often said that the credibility of an actor can be judged by how convincingly they play an inebriated character. Unfortunately in a couple of the MGM features we can see Buster attempting to play sober when drunk, but happily there are a couple of delightful instances of the converse, where he plays an individual who's had a couple too many. A highlight of *Three Ages* has him innocently drinking a pitcher of bootleg booze in the belief that it's plain water, and quickly becoming unknowingly blotto. He underplays every moment, and the end of the scene, where he stumbles into a taxi, falls straight out of the other door, pays the bewildered driver and wanders off into the night, is an absolute joy.

Stories of Buster the man are rife with his generosity and lack of ego. Buster would always put himself second to his involvement with the task in hand – be it shooting a scene or winning a game of baseball. Two examples come to mind, both related by Rudi Blesh in his biography *Keaton*.

A number of Buster's stunts were literally death-defying, but maybe his closest brush with death came while filming *Our Hospitality*. In trying to save his leading lady, played by his wife Natalie, our hero has fallen into the Truckee river and is hurtling towards rapids. He is attached to an unseen hold-back wire to prevent him being swept away. The wire has been rigged up by his trusty technical director Fred Gabourie – all Buster has to do is to allow himself to be carried along. Unfortunately the wire snaps and Buster is suddenly careering out of control in the fast-moving current. He is hitting his knees, hips and chest against the rocks, with the water threatening to crush him against a boulder. Only a bend in the river saves him and he eventually manages to pull himself exhausted onto the bank. Tellingly his first thought is whether Natalie witnessed it, quickly followed by whether it had been captured on film. Gabourie took full blame for the accident and offered to resign on the spot. Buster wouldn't hear of it. As Blesh relates it, "Buster put a wet arm around Gabe's shoulder. 'You'll never make another mistake,' he said. Gabouri never did."

Rudi Blesh also related a conversation with Buster's long-time writing partner Clyde Bruckman, who revealed that although Buster's name seldom appeared on the screen as writer, the wonderful stories that were credited to Bruckman or to Jean Havez were "ninety percent Buster's". Bruckman was ashamed to take the money, and much less the credit. But when he tried to tell Buster so, Buster just laughed and told him to stick around. "I need a left fielder." Bruckman summed up working with the man he called "Bus": "Harold Lloyd was wonderful to me. So was [W.C.] Fields. But with Bus you belonged."

So it's clear that whatever life threw at him, Buster would be able to keep things in proportion – as long as he was given sufficient control. He realised that the business of film-making needs time to breathe, and so if the creative juices weren't flowing, or a gag seemed to get stuck, or even if it was simply that the time seemed right, then he would grab the opportunity to indulge in another of his great passions, baseball. It didn't escape the attention of film commentators at the time that Buster employed a suspiciously high number of baseball players. A joke Keaton Productions application form appeared in the press:

Are you a good actor?	Yes ☐	No ☐
Are you a good baseball player?	Yes ☐	No ☐
Passing grade: 50%		

But Buster could use baseball as a useful weapon to call upon when his creativity was being undermined. When making *College*, he had a new studio manager foisted on him, Harry Brand. Brand immediately rubbed Buster up the wrong way when he began to prioritise finance over art. On one occasion, although Snitz Edwards had finished his scenes in the film, Buster wanted him to stick around in case inspiration struck and further scenes needed to be shot. But Brand immediately took Edwards off the payroll without telling Buster. Buster's response was to effectively go on strike – by gathering the crew and playing baseball for three days straight.

Ernie Orsatti was part of Buster's crew from 1923 onwards, first as a stunt-man and then part of the art department. Buster noticed his prowess at base-ball and encouraged him to take it up professionally. In 1927 Orsatti signed with the St Louis Cardinals, and went on to win two World Series finals with the team.

In film making terms, it's now clear that Buster was very much ahead of his time. His reputation among those who don't really know his work is of an over-the-top, custard pie flinging clown who would tumble and twirl at the drop of a porkpie hat. Nothing could be further from the truth. Of course, his shorts feature slapstick to a greater or lesser extent, and naturally physical comedy – including the (very) occasionally flung item of foodstuff – would always pre-vail over verbal, but almost without exception his silent films have a depth and sophistication that belie their origins.

He later said that he only disagreed with his good friend and mentor Roscoe Arbuckle in one respect. Roscoe's advice to him when making a film was to treat the audience as if they were twelve years old. This may be the result of Roscoe having started in the film industry several years before Buster, but Buster realised that audience tastes were developing, and to play down to them would be a mistake. For all Roscoe's skill and charm, for modern audiences his performances are often let down by a surfeit of mugging and winking at the camera, over-playing his part and making sure nothing is lost on the audience. Buster was aware that even after just a decade or so of cinema-going, audi-ences were more sophisticated than Roscoe gave them credit for. So much so that we can watch Buster's films now, some 100 years later, and the comedy is still fresh, the ideas still relevant, and his performances, albeit in the context of hand-cranked silent filming, still enthralling. Whereas Roscoe's technique for taking the audience with him was to grab us by the scruff of the neck and haul us along after him, Buster might flash a brief enigmatic glance, pause for half a second and then set off on his own. We follow, utterly beguiled and desperate to know what he's about to do.

Indeed, if we look back over Buster's catalogue of work it is interesting to note that what we would today see as the pinnacle of his achievement – in par-ticular the miraculous triumvirate of *Sherlock Jr.*, *The General* and *Steamboat Bill, Jr.* – were not as well received as we might expect. And what now seem to be rather embarrassing time-fillers, such as a number of the Educational and even the Columbia shorts, were on the whole still very well received by the public.

Technically also, Buster was innovative in being an early proponent of shooting his films (largely) at the correct speed. Silent comedies were often shot with the film being turned a little slowly – called "under-cranking" – so that when projected at the correct speed the action would appear sped up, artificially frantic and unnaturally madcap. Buster realised that the gags would work best if taken at the correct speed, so that attention would be focussed on the gag itself rather than the fact that everything is zipping along at breakneck pace. This is not to say he never under-cranked of course – it came in very handy for upping the excitement of chase scenes, for example – but much of his physical comedy is filmed at pretty much the correct speed. As such, his timing is impeccable. The merest pause accompanied by a slight shift in weight, or a quick double take – his performances are thoroughly captivating.

We must lay one particular myth to rest, however – that of Buster as the Great Stone Face. There is a world of difference between someone who rarely smiles and someone whose face expresses no emotion. Buster's rarely smiling face is a wellspring of emotion. Blessed with what critic Penelope Houston called "apprehensive good looks", Buster has a face that is truly mesmerising. Every expression is a precious gift, often understated but always perfectly judged. A slight furrowing of the brow when plans go inexplicably awry. A brief but gorgeous fluttering of the eyelids when catching the scent of his seemingly unapproachable love interest. A sidelong glance in anticipation of the next misfortune to foil his plans. A fleeting hesitation … Those perpetuating the Great Stone Face myth only need watch *The Playhouse*. The beautifully judged interplay between the members of the audience – all played by Buster – are astonishing enough in their timing and authenticity, but his precise yet subtle mimicry of the ape in the second reel shows just what a lovely work of art Buster's supremely adaptable face is.

Critic James Agee put it perfectly – "Keaton's face ranked almost with Lincoln's as an early American archetype; it was haunting, handsome, almost beautiful, yet it was irreducibly funny".

Buster was always happy to explain the origins of the non-smiling persona that he had developed. It went back to the days of vaudeville, where experience – and his father – quickly taught him that the audience found a gag much funnier if, rather than laugh along with them, he expressed mild bemusement while being slightly hurt to think that anyone would take pleasure at his misfortune.

But we can guess that this performance trait was pretty much an extension of Buster's own character. As a child he seems to have been quietly inquisitive, more interested in finding out how the world worked than seeking its approbation. And not really one to make a fuss – from falling down a full flight of stairs aged two, or needing the tip of a finger amputated after coming off second best when exploring the mechanism of a clothes mangle aged three, we can easily imagine him seeing such adversity as simply part of life's rich tapestry of experience.

One unintended side effect of never smiling was the assumption by some over-protective members of his vaudeville audience that Buster was being abused. He remembers his father being hauled in front of three successive mayors of New York on grounds of suspected cruelty, and young Buster being stripped and searched for signs of sprains, bruising or broken bones. They were always disappointed. Child labour laws forbade children engaging in singing, dancing, juggling or acrobatics. But, as Buster would fondly recall, nothing about them being hit over the head or thrown across the stage. One hopefully not apocryphal tale from the Keaton annals relates how a child protection officer came backstage looking for underage performers. "How about that little fellow in the tumbling act?" he asked the stage manager. "I dunno," the stage manager replied. And, pointing to Buster's mother Myra, he suggested, "Ask his wife!"

Buster's life story is told elsewhere – in *Tempest in a Flat Hat*, a loving biography by Edward McPherson, in astonishing depth in James Curtis' *Buster Keaton: A Filmmaker's Life*, and most superbly in the three-part documentary *A Hard Act to Follow* by Kevin Brownlow and David Gill. There is a touching aside by Kevin Brownlow on the subject of his documentary in his "Afterword" to the book *Buster Keaton Remembered* by Eleanor Keaton and Jeffrey Vance –

> "When one embarks upon a biographical documentary, one is liable to uncover some unpleasant facts about the subject. After we had finished the Keaton film, however, we realized that we had found no one who had a single unkind word to say about the man – and this was a fellow who had gone through a rough period of alcoholism. All those who knew him seemed to have loved him."

A Hard Act to Follow, which includes an extensive interview with Eleanor Keaton, is absolutely required viewing. But meanwhile, for a two-reel overview of the life of Buster Keaton –

Buster was born in 1895, the eldest child of vaudevillians Joe and Myra. He acquired his nickname as a toddler after tumbling unhurt down a flight of stairs, prompting a family friend – who Buster would always identify as Harry Houdini, but was most likely the British-born comedian and manager George A. Pardey – to comment how that was "some buster", vaudeville slang for a fall. The name stuck. He joined his parents' stage act in 1900, and The Three Keatons became famous for the physicality of their knockabout routines, Buster stoically accepting being flung by his father across the stage, into the scenery, into the audience. With the arrival of Buster's younger brother "Jingles" the act sporadically became The Four Keatons, and then with Louise even more sporadically Five, but the essence continued to be Joe, Myra and Buster.

Joe was unimpressed with the movie industry, but Buster was curious and in 1917 a chance meeting with Roscoe "Fatty" Arbuckle, one of the industry's top comedians, started him on the road in a series of short films. In 1920 he began making his own shorts, progressing to feature films in 1923.

He was at the top of his game until circumstances (more to do with the emergence of the Hollywood studio system than the oft-cited advent of sound), and poor if well-meant advice, led him to give up the independence of Buster Keaton Productions to join MGM in 1928, one of the few decisions in his life that he would later bitterly regret – and indeed call the relevant chapter in his autobiography "The Worst Mistake of My Life". Joe Schenck, who had been Buster's producer from day one, had always had total faith in Buster and had become like a guardian angel, giving him complete artistic freedom to create his series of masterful movies without having to worry about where the money would come from. He was also Buster's brother-in-law, being married to Norma Talmadge, sister of Buster's first wife Natalie Talmadge. But now Schenck was also president of United Artists, and, probably taking his eye off the ball as far as Buster was concerned, also recommended that he throw his lot in with MGM, which must have swayed Buster more than somewhat. However, Schenck continued to give Buster discreet but substantial financial support in the lean years to come.

Because MGM didn't know how to handle Buster, and their tightly budgeted formula for film making was diametrically opposed to Buster's unscripted, freewheeling, opportunistic working methods. Although commercially successful, his MGM films were artistically stifling, and Buster took to drink. He hit rock bottom in 1933 when his twelve-year marriage to Natalie Talmadge ended, his alcohol consumption peaked, his MGM contract was suddenly terminated and his good friend Roscoe Arbuckle died. To add insult to injury, Natalie then changed the names of Buster's two boys from Keaton to Talmadge, a change that was made official in May 1942. This clearly hurt Buster very deeply, to the point that Natalie is not mentioned in his 1960 autobiography *My Wonderful World of Slapstick*.

Always committed to taking on whatever work was offered, in 1934 he signed up with Educational Pictures to make a series of low-budget shorts, followed by a similarly largely disappointing series of shorts for Columbia in 1939–41. His life began to turn around in 1940 when he married Eleanor Norris, a devoted partner, devout companion and staunch ally who was by his side for the rest of his life.

Throughout the 1940s, Buster's career entered into something of a freewheeling phase, as he was employed by various studios as an uncredited screenwriter on films such as *Tales of Manhattan* for Twentieth Century-Fox, and played cameo roles in the likes of Universal's *San Diego, I Love You*.

A key article by critic James Agee in *Life* magazine on 5 September 1949 praising the talents of the big four silent comedians – Charlie Chaplin and the then largely forgotten Harold Lloyd, Harry Langdon and Buster Keaton

– triggered Buster's artistic renaissance. By the end of the year he was working on his own TV series.

He appeared in two key films of the early 1950s with echoes of the silent era, *Sunset Boulevard* with Gloria Swanson and *Limelight* with Chaplin, raising his profile and leading to a series of cameo roles in feature films such as *Around the World in 80 Days*, *The Adventures of Huckleberry Finn* and *It's a Mad, Mad, Mad, Mad World*.

Fate was on his side as regards his place in film history. The vast majority of silent films no longer exist – the Martin Scorsese Film Foundation estimates that more than 90% of American films made before 1929 are lost – but by a stroke of luck, all but one of Buster's silents are available today. In the early 1950s, the British actor James Mason, who had bought Buster's old 1920s home, the "Italian villa", chanced upon a stash of his films hidden in an outhouse in the grounds. This find – discovered just in time, as the unstable nitrate film stock was starting to decompose – formed the basis for the restoration of Buster's entire canon of silent films.

As such, and thanks to his star being once again on the rise, movie audiences began to rediscover these old silent shorts and happily Buster lived long enough to see his glorious silent films fully applauded once more by critics, and embraced by an enthusiastic young audience.

And so, let's start at the very beginning …

Jos. M. Schenck presents
FATTY ARBUCKLE
and
THE WORLD'S BEST
COMEDY ORGANIZATION
Al. St. John
Comedian
Buster Keaton
Comedian
Fatty Arbuckle
Alice Lake
Comedienne
Paramount Program
Herbert Warren
Scenarios
Lou Anger
Business Manager
Paul Conlon
Personal Press Representative
George Peters
Photographer

The Butcher Boy

Directed by: Roscoe "Fatty" Arbuckle
Produced by: Joseph M. Schenck
Presented by: Joseph M. Schenck
Written by: Roscoe "Fatty" Arbuckle, Joseph Anthony Roach
Released: 23 April 1917
Length: 24 minutes (2 reels)

Cast:
Roscoe "Fatty" Arbuckle – The butcher boy
Buster Keaton – The village pest
Al St. John – Slim, the clerk
Josephine Stevens – Almondine, cashier
Arthur Earle – Mr. Grouch, the proprietor
Joe Bordeaux – Accomplice
Agnes Neilson – Miss Teachem, principal of seminary
Luke – The dog
Charles Dudley
Alice Lake

Cinematography: Frank D. Williams
Edited by: Herbert Warren
Production company: Comique Films
Distributed by: Paramount Pictures

It's chaos as usual at Grouch's General Store. Slim scales the dizzy heights of incompetence in the store and Fatty uses all his ingenuity to short-change customers at the butcher's counter. Add Buster to the mix, turning up to buy a tinful of molasses, and all hell breaks loose. Tension heightens between Fatty and Slim over their love for the cashier, Mr. Grouch's daughter Almondine. To nip this in the bud, Mr. Grouch sends her to Miss Teachem's school for girls. Undeterred Fatty and Slim independently don female attire to enrol at the boarding school. Fatty and Almondine, aided by Luke the dog, slip away from the ensuing mayhem in search of a parson.

In New York in March 1917, probably a Monday and possibly the 19th, Buster happened to run into a friend of the Keatons from their vaudeville days, Lou Anger, who had in the meantime moved into the movie world and was managing Joseph M. Schenck's film enterprises. (Some sources report that it was Schenck himself who Buster ran into.) In any event, the chance meeting resulted in an introduction to Roscoe "Fatty" Arbuckle, who as a comic actor was second only to Charlie Chaplin in terms of popularity with movie-goers at the time. The upshot of the meeting was that Buster turned down a $250 a week engagement in *The Passing Show of 1917* at the Winter Garden Theatre in favour of earning $40 a week (or so Buster always claimed) for appearing in movies, starting with what happened to be the first film from Arbuckle's new Comique (pronounced Com-*ee*-kay) Film Corporation, *The Butcher Boy*.

Filming took place in Joe Schenck's studios on East 48th St between First and Second Avenues. At the same time and in the same loft space, the famous Talmadge sisters, Norma and Constance, were each filming separate feature-length productions. Buster would claim that his first appearance was the only newcomer's debut comedy scene that was filmed only once – in other words his first ever scene on film did not need a retake.

It's worth repeating that Roscoe was a huge star at the time, and his break from the Mack Sennett fold and launch of his solo career was met with tremendous anticipation. *Moving Picture World* reported that Paramount had made deals for simultaneous showings of his first film with over 35 theatres in New York alone, and the company's national promotional work "will outstrip anything of its kind ever attempted in the industry". Nationally, the film's initial print run was increased from 75 to 200, and profits were such that Roscoe was on track to earn $1 million (around $20 million today) in his first year.

This meant that Buster's debut received far more attention than would have been the case if he'd appeared alongside almost anyone else, and even had he joined Roscoe a year or two down the line. All eyes were on Roscoe, anticipating his first solo short, and into this frenzy of scrutiny stepped 21-year-old Buster.

Of course, Roscoe's star would rise even higher with these shorts with Buster. It reached the point where the two-reelers, which were designed to support a feature length film, became the sole attraction. And even when they did support a feature, the short film could receive top billing.

And a further note – Buster quickly became Roscoe's creative equal, and so effectively was co-director and co-writer of most of their shorts. However, we've kept the credit with Roscoe as the exact contributions of each have of course been lost in the mists of time.

Roscoe's first post-Sennett film continues the template of many a Mack Sennett two-reeler: choose a setting, introduce characters, and create chaos around various rivals in love. Then choose a new setting and repeat for reel two.

For the memorable early scene where Roscoe throws a bag of flour knocking Buster off his feet, he realised that it would be virtually impossible to do this without Buster flinching. He therefore told Buster to be facing the other way and to turn around when he called "turn". Roscoe's aim and timing were perfect and Buster catches the flour full in the face, executing a spectacular fall, putting his neck and shoulders where his feet had been, and vice versa.

The film also contains one of the few occasions on which Buster is seen to fling a custard pie.

The names of the characters in the film are curiously fluid, varying between different prints of the film, contemporary reviews and current DVD releases. Roscoe's character is variously "Fatty", "Saccharine" and "the butcher boy". Al St. John is billed as "Alum" and "clerk", and on the Eureka Masters of Cinema DVD collection as "Slim Snavely, sales manager". The DVD also credits Josephine Stevens as "Amanda" and Arthur Earle as "Mr. Grouch", otherwise "Almondine" and "the store manager" respectively. According to *Variety*, Agnes Neilson's character's full name is "Lemmy Teachem".

A Reckless Romeo

Directed by: Roscoe "Fatty" Arbuckle
Produced by: Joseph M. Schenck
Presented by: Joseph M. Schenck
Written by: Roscoe "Fatty" Arbuckle, Joseph Anthony Roach
Released: 21 May 1917
Length: 23 minutes (2 reels)

Cast:
Roscoe "Fatty" Arbuckle – The husband
Buster Keaton – Blind beggarwoman (unconfirmed)
Corinne Parquet – The wife
Agnes Neilson – The mother-in-law
Alice Lake – The pretty girl in the park
Al St. John – The pretty girl's boyfriend
Jimmy Bryant – The newsreel director

Cinematography: Frank D. Williams
Edited by: Herbert Warren
Production company: Comique Films
Distributed by: Paramount Pictures

To appease his wife and mother-in-law after arriving home drunk at 3 am, Fatty takes them on a Sunday evening walk around Palisades Park. While alone, he cannot contain his philandering ways, resulting in a fist fight with the boyfriend of a girl who catches his eye. By chance, the fight is caught on film by a roving newsreel reporter who is out to expose "mashers flirting in our parks". Ignorant of having been filmed, Fatty explains to his beloved that his black eye is as a result of coming to the rescue of a blind beggarwoman. Some time later, the happy trio retire to the theatre. Unfortunately the newsreel is part of that night's entertainment, and, worse still, the girl and her boyfriend are also in the audience.

A Reckless Romeo was thought lost until the Norwegian Film Archive discovered a copy in an unmarked canister in 1998.

It is included here, although it is by no means certain that it should be. Although definitely released on 21 May 1917, it is likely that this wasn't filmed as the follow-up to *The Butcher Boy*. It is felt by many to be Roscoe's last Keystone film from 1916 which was sold to Paramount to fulfil his release schedule, or was completed after Roscoe set up Comique Film Corporation in January 1917. As such, Buster's participation is, of course, questionable, as he first met Roscoe in March 1917. Unusually and unhelpfully, there appears to be no copyright on the film, so there is no copyright date to help us.

If Buster does appear in the film, his role is not obvious. While the film was considered lost, it was either omitted from Buster's filmographies or he was credited with the wrong character ("rival" or "newsreel reporter", for example). Now we can see the film, the only possibility is that he is heavily disguised as the blind beggarwoman (who turns out not to be blind of course). We see her in close up, and from what we see of the face it could conceivably be Buster, and certainly the stature and physicality do not rule him out, but the actor does seem to be rather too old.

The clincher could be a report in *Moving Picture World* on 30 September 1916 – while Roscoe was still with Keystone and before he and Buster had met. This includes news that Roscoe was winding up shooting of his latest film, and describes in detail how the studio had been transformed into the interior of a theatre, complete with proscenium arch, a 20-piece orchestra and banks of palms – all of which feature in the finale of the released *A Reckless Romeo*. So if Buster is indeed the beggarwoman, the whole flashback sequence in which the beggarwoman appears would have to have been shot much later, in 1917 – which seems highly unlikely. Even less likely is that Buster's scenes were cut from the final release.

So the smart money should certainly go on Buster *not* appearing in the picture.

And yet ... Buster's biography in the 1918 *Motion Picture Studio Directory and Trade Annual* includes *A Reckless Romeo* among his credits. And although the film is not mentioned in Rudi Blesh's 1966 biography, written with Buster's cooperation, it is in the filmography section of Eleanor Keaton's later tribute *Buster Keaton Remembered*.

The exteriors were indeed filmed in Palisades Park, which at the time was owned by the Schenck brothers. Joe Bordeaux is sometimes credited, though doesn't seem to appear in the film.

The Rough House

Directed by: Roscoe "Fatty" Arbuckle
Produced by: Joseph M. Schenck
Presented by: Joseph M. Schenck
Written by: Roscoe "Fatty" Arbuckle, Joseph Anthony Roach
Released: 25 June 1917
Length: 19 minutes (2 reels)

Cast:
Roscoe "Fatty" Arbuckle – Mr. Rough
Buster Keaton – Gardener / Delivery boy / Cop
Al St. John – Cook
Alice Lake – Mrs. Rough
Agnes Neilson – Mother-in-law
Joe Bordeaux – Police officer (unconfirmed)
Josephine Stevens – Maid

Cinematography: Frank D. Williams
Edited by: Herbert Warren
Production company: Comique Films
Distributed by: Paramount Pictures

> In the house of Mr. and Mrs. Rough, the day begins with customary chaos when Fatty sets fire to his bed. Having put out the fire with a high power garden hose, he forcibly evicts his cook and a delivery boy who have been fighting for the affections of the maid. The pair are immediately arrested but avoid jail by agreeing to join the understaffed police force. When two guests at the Rough house are later spotted robbing their hosts, the erstwhile cook and delivery boy are despatched on the case for a decidedly Keystone Kops-style second reel.

It's a measure of Buster's ability to learn and to develop – not to mention his inventiveness – as much as it is of Roscoe's generosity in sharing his expertise and his openness to accepting new ideas and influences, that it can be said that we're just two films in and already the Arbuckle shorts have become the Arbuckle–Keaton shorts. In *The Rough House* we can see clear signs of Buster as co-director and co-writer.

A passing moment that resonates with modern audiences has Roscoe entertaining the maid by sticking forks into a couple of bread rolls and doing a little side-kicking stroll along the table. Eight years later this would become the memorable so-called "Oceana Dance" sequence in Charlie Chaplin's *The Gold Rush* – in fact it is one of Chaplin's most iconic scenes. It is interesting to speculate who originated the idea. Did Chaplin see it in *The Rough House* and store it away for later use? Or had Chaplin already tried it out in an idle moment when he and Arbuckle had worked together in the Sennett days back in 1914, and it was Arbuckle who "borrowed" the idea? Either way, the two incarnations work extremely well and are both beautifully judged – Roscoe uses it as a throwaway bit of nonsense designed to add to Mrs. Rough's irritation, and Chaplin expands it into a bravura performance of exquisite inventiveness.

Roscoe with
Josephine Stevens

Many modern viewers like to pinpoint "the only time Buster Keaton smiles on film". Usually they cite the test-your-strength sequence in *Coney Island*, but, particularly in the earlier films, Buster often laughs. He briefly shows his delight when Mr. Grouch is upended by a thrown pie in *The Butcher Boy*, but his first full-on outburst of hysteria occurs half-way through *The Rough House*, when Roscoe throws a pan of sticky dough over Al St. John. Buster is delighted, clapping his hands with glee. He is still cracking a smile as late as in *The Garage*.

There is also a tribute to Joe Keaton's trademark high kicks towards the end of the film when Buster fells a postman with a spectacular high kick of his own.

After brief appearances in *The Butcher Boy* and *A Reckless Romeo*, Alice Lake makes her mark in this Arbuckle–Keaton short. She became a staple of the series before leaving for Metro in 1919. She was a talented comedienne, and by all accounts something of a free spirit, not averse to dancing topless on set between takes. Her uninhibited performance in *Good Night, Nurse!* is probably as close as we get to a glimpse of her true nature.

His Wedding Night

Directed by: Roscoe "Fatty" Arbuckle
Produced by: Joseph M. Schenck
Presented by: Joseph M. Schenck
Written by: Roscoe "Fatty" Arbuckle, Joseph Anthony Roach
Released: 20 August 1917
Length: 19 minutes (2 reels)

Cast:
Roscoe "Fatty" Arbuckle – Drugstore soda clerk
Buster Keaton – Delivery boy
Al St. John – Rival suitor
Alice Mann – Alice
Arthur Earle – Justice of the Peace
Joe Bordeaux – Accomplice
Jimmy Bryant – Accomplice
Josephine Stevens – Customer
Alice Lake – Perfume customer
Natalie Talmadge – Pretty lady in the car

Cinematography: George Peters
Edited by: Herbert Warren
Production company: Comique Films
Distributed by: Paramount Pictures

We're in the Koff and Kramp drugstore, and once again Fatty and Al are vying for the hand of the boss's daughter Alice. Having done his best to sell perfume at $4 an ounce, Fatty is called outside on petrol pump duties. Al seizes his chance, but Alice stops him in his tracks by pointing out that the ring on her finger has been put there by Fatty. Down but not out, Al persuades his cohorts to help him kidnap Alice. Meanwhile Buster arrives with Alice's much anticipated wedding gown. For reasons of plot, he models it for her. When her back is turned, Al turns up and kidnaps the begowned one, assuming it to be Alice, by throwing a bag over her head. He heads straight for the Justice of the Peace and demands that he marry them. Happily before any problematic same-sex marriage can take place, Fatty turns up, dispatches the kidnappers and instructs the Justice to marry him to the still-hooded bride. Once again catastrophe is averted as the real Alice turns up in the nick of time, the hood is removed and all confusion is cleared up. The film ends as the smiling newlyweds walk away, leaving us in the dark as to what actually happens on His Wedding Night.

The film contains an unusually high number of rather suspect scenes – Fatty as the soda clerk (as they were then known) drugs a female customer so that he can kiss her, a highly effeminate customer delights in dousing himself in lady's perfume with Fatty providing a bathtub for the purpose, and Fatty sells a black woman charcoal instead of face cream. Not to mention the film's forays into what contemporary audiences would have come to expect from their comedy shorts – namely topics such as kidnap, extortion, transvestism, racketeering and a shotgun marriage.

Such themes were relished by the press – the review in *Moving Picture World* describes Buster as "the sissy who has delivered the bridal gown and who has put it on to show how it hangs".

In one scene, Roscoe attends to a chauffeur-driven Rolls Royce (quickly raising the advertised price of gasoline from 26c to $1 as the car draws up). It has been suggested that one of the passengers in the car is Virginia Rappe, the actress at the centre of the 1921 scandal that effectively finished Roscoe's career (see p. 61 for details). This is certainly possible as there is a strong resemblance, though it is possibly too much of a coincidence. The car, incidentally, was Roscoe's own, a present from Joe Schenck when he branched out on his own.

It had been announced back in April 1917 that *His Wedding Night*, written by Herbert Warren and William Jefferson, would be Roscoe's second short, the follow-up to *The Butcher Boy*.

The boisterous nature of the Comique two-reelers was hampering the more serious business of filming dramas in the same studio space on East 48th Street – as was mentioned earlier, while *The Butcher Boy* was being shot, Norma and Constance Talmadge were each trying to concentrate on filming separate feature-length dramas. And so for this film and the subsequent one, Roscoe & co. moved uptown to studio space rented from Biograph on 174th Street in the Bronx.

Oh Doctor!

Directed by: Roscoe "Fatty" Arbuckle
Produced by: Joseph M. Schenck
Presented by: Joseph M. Schenck
Written by: Jean Havez, Joseph Anthony Roach
Released: 30 September 1917
Length: 23 minutes (2 reels)

Cast:
Roscoe "Fatty" Arbuckle – Doctor
Buster Keaton – Doctor's son
Alice Lake – Doctor's wife
Al St. John – Gambler

Alice Mann – Maid
Joe Bordeaux – Tipster / Cop
Joseph Anthony Roach (unconfirmed)

Cinematography: George Peters
Edited by: Herbert Warren
Production company: Comique Films
Distributed by: Paramount Pictures

A day at the races with the Holepokes. Doctor Fatty, flirting with a woman, overhears her feckless gambler of a boyfriend share a hot tip. The horse fails to finish and Fatty and the gambler lose heavily. To avoid ruin, the gambler decides to recoup his losses at the expense of the well-to-do doctor. Wrongs are happily righted thanks to the appearance in the plot of an outsized policeman's uniform and the unwitting ingenuity of the doctor's surprisingly grown-up-looking son.

Jean Havez joined the Arbuckle–Keaton team for the first time on *Oh Doctor!*, being mainly responsible for the intertitles. He would write three more Arbuckle–Keaton shorts before teaming up with Clyde Bruckman and Joseph Mitchell to form Buster's dream team of writers for his first five features.

Although the title cards of some current versions of the short give Roscoe's character the name of Dr. Holepoke, this may have been a recent invention. Contemporary reviews, such as in *Moving Picture World*, identify the character as Dr. I.O. Dine. One enterprising theatre owner created a calling card for the good doctor.

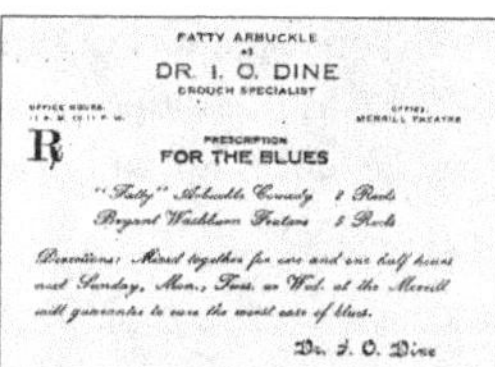

This is Buster's least deadpan performance. Playing a histrionic teenager, he laughs, he cries, he sulks, he charms, he irritates, he gets walloped … And one reviewer's imagination just couldn't stretch far enough – the *Motion Picture News* correspondent explains how Mr. Arbuckle goes to the races with his wife and her brother.

Roscoe and Buster with Alice Lake

Coney Island

Aka *Fatty at Coney Island*

Directed by: Roscoe "Fatty" Arbuckle
Produced by: Joseph M. Schenck
Presented by: Joseph M. Schenck
Written by: Roscoe "Fatty" Arbuckle
Released: 29 October 1917
Length: 25 minutes (2 reels)

Cast:
Roscoe "Fatty" Arbuckle – Fatty
Agnes Neilson – Fatty's wife
Al St. John – Old friend of Fatty's wife
Buster Keaton – Rival / Cop with oversize moustache
Alice Mann – The girl
Joe Bordeaux – Ticket seller / Cop
Jimmy Bryant – Test-your-strength operator
Alice Lake
Natalie Talmadge – Soda kiosk customer
Luke – The dog

Cinematography: George Peters
Edited by: Herbert Warren
Production company: Comique Films
Distributed by: Paramount Pictures

Buster takes his girl to the Coney Island fun fair. Fatty, having given his wife the slip, has a run-in with Buster over the test-your-strength machine. Meanwhile Fatty's wife runs into a young friend and asks him to help find her husband. The friend instead steals Buster's girl, only to have her stolen from him by Fatty. The love pentagon plays out on the beach with Fatty stealing a large woman's bathing suit as nothing else will fit him, enabling him to flaunt his drag skills, while Buster gets a job as a life guard, enabling him impress us with a spurious back flip. Buster ends up with the girl, Fatty and his wife's friend end up athletically fighting it out in a prison cell before calling a truce, sealing a pact, and contriving to lock Mrs. Fatty in the cell.

Buster later told Rudi Blesh of an incident that occurred during filming, which is particularly telling in light of the terrible events surrounding Roscoe in 1921 (see p. 61). On the third day of shooting Roscoe announced reshooting was needed as a female extra was no longer with them. She had come into his dressing room with two bathing costumes, asking which she should wear. She drops one, then the other, revealing herself to be naked. "So you *fired* her," Buster said. "Are you nuts?" Roscoe replied that he had the sense to get straight out of there, and had all but knocked her mother down outside the dressing room. "She was all set to bust in. Daughter would scream. Ma would yell, 'Rape!' And here would come Pa with the shotgun."

Much of the film was shot on location at Luna Park, Coney Island. It is notable for being a particularly character-driven presentation, and less of a string of gags loosely strung together, with the Coney Island amusement park providing scope for a range of slapstick set-pieces. There is also a pleasing arc to the story, with Buster ending up back with his girl.

Buster doubles up as one of the cops, thinly disguised in an unconvincing moustache, and also doubles for Alice Mann when she and Roscoe are thrown out of the water chute. Natalie Talmadge may also appear in the film.

The final shot is happily cut from nearly every print of the film – Roscoe pursues a woman and, on catching up with her and seeing that she is black, flees in terror.

A Country Hero

Directed by: Roscoe "Fatty" Arbuckle
Produced by: Joseph M. Schenck
Presented by: Joseph M. Schenck
Written by: Roscoe "Fatty" Arbuckle
Released: 10 December 1917
Length: 2 reels

Cast:
Roscoe "Fatty" Arbuckle – Village blacksmith
Buster Keaton – Fatima, vaudeville artist
Al St. John – City gent
Alice Lake – Schoolteacher
Joe Keaton – Cy Klone, garage owner
Stanley Pembroke
Natalie Talmadge

Cinematography: George Peters
Edited by: Herbert Warren
Production company: Comique Films
Distributed by: Paramount Pictures

> *As the film is currently lost, we can only get a synopsis from contemporary reviews and articles on the production.*
>
> The scene is the rural village of Jazzville where blacksmith Fatty and owner of the Spark Plug Garage, Cy Klone, battle for the affections of the local schoolteacher. The rivals join forces when a common enemy arrives in the form of a suave city type who moves in on the girl and whisks her off to the city. Meanwhile, in a twist on a snake-charming act, vaudeville artist Fatima bewitches one and all by charming a long black stocking from a cigar box. Things soon get out of hand however, and Fatty starts hurling pianos around. The latter part of the action sees Fatty in pursuit of the city slicker, resulting in at least one Ford motor car being destroyed by a locomotive.

A Country Hero was the first Comique film to be shot after the company moved to California, and the first with Joe Keaton. Curiously, in the excellent biography *Keaton*, written in 1966 with Buster's help by his friend Rudi Blesh, *A Country Hero* is listed as the penultimate Arbuckle–Keaton movie, released in 1920. This error probably derives from the fact that, for reasons unknown, the film was not copyrighted until 20 December 1920 – almost a year after the release of Buster and Roscoe's last film.

With the film currently lost, we cannot confirm the cast list, either in terms of characters or of actors taking part, although the listing above is probably the best guess. (Natalie Talmadge's participation is confirmed in a paragraph in *Photoplay* of March 1918.) Roscoe undoubtedly plays the blacksmith, and Alice Lake the schoolteacher. Buster is the wriggling Fatima, bewitching all and sundry. The garage owner, Cy Klone, is probably played by Joe Keaton, although the film's review in *Variety* describes Joe as a "storekeeper". Then again, Rudi Blesh explains how Roscoe suggested that Joe, for his screen debut, could play the schoolteacher's father, a deal that was apparently sealed when Alice Lake told Joe that she was perfectly happy for him to execute his renowned high kicks on her. This is not to say, of course, that the schoolma'am's father couldn't also be a storekeeper, but this would safely rule out Joe playing Cy Klone, which would make him both Alice Lake's father and her suitor. The studio press release discloses that Roscoe, Buster and Al St. John combine forces to get a car to shift from the Spark Plug Garage – although Al St. John playing the city type seems most likely. In fact, stills from the film show him in a pair of rather fetching checked trousers.

Press still featuring Al St. John

Out West

Directed by: Roscoe "Fatty" Arbuckle
Produced by: Joseph M. Schenck
Presented by: Joseph M. Schenck
Written by: Roscoe "Fatty" Arbuckle, Natalie Talmadge
Released: 20 January 1918
Length: 21 minutes (2 reels)

Cast:
Roscoe "Fatty" Arbuckle – Train rider, bartender
Buster Keaton – Bill Bullhorn, saloon owner
Al St. John – Wild Bill Hickup
Alice Lake – Salvation Army woman
Joe Keaton – Guard on train
Ernie Morrison Sr. – Black man

Cinematography: George Peters
Edited by: Herbert Warren
Production company: Comique Films
Distributed by: Paramount Pictures

Fatty is kicked off the train that he's been stowing away on, and finds himself in the desert. His bulk soon attracts the interest of a group of American Indians and he flees to the nearest settlement. Storming into town he thwarts a hold-up of the saloon by Wild Bill Hickup, earning him the job of bartender. A suddenly shocking scene where a black man is forced to bullet dance ends when he is saved by a Salvation Army worker. Fatty quickly falls for her of course, and so is first out of the blocks when Wild Bill Hickup kidnaps her in revenge.

The idea for the script came from Buster's future wife, Natalie Talmadge, who was the script editor on the film.

Buster had form in satirising the western – he and Joe had developed similar routines in their vaudeville act, parodying the overwrought melodrama of westerns of the time.

The film's realism is astonishingly dark, featuring at least eight deaths, racism against blacks and Native Americans that is quite shocking by today's standards, and conversely Natives declaring that killing Fatty would provide much food for the winter. Only Fatty is even vaguely sympathetic. And at the same time the film is quite fantastical with the arch villain being overcome – repeatedly – by tickling.

Scenes were shot at the Horkheimer brothers' Balboa Amusement Producing Company Studios in Long Beach, California, and at the gloriously named Mad Dog Gulch in San Gabriel Canyon, near Los Angeles.

Some sources date the film's release as 20 February 1918, but this is the date it was registered for copyright.

The Bell Boy

Directed by: Roscoe "Fatty" Arbuckle
Produced by: Joseph M. Schenck
Presented by: Joseph M. Schenck
Written by: Roscoe "Fatty" Arbuckle
Released: 18 March 1918
Length: 26 minutes (2, possibly 3 reels)

Cast:
Roscoe "Fatty" Arbuckle – Bell boy, barber
Buster Keaton – Bell boy
Al St. John – Desk clerk
Alice Lake – Cutie Cuticle, manicurist
Joe Keaton – Guest
Charles Dudley – Guest (Rasputin the Mystic)

Cinematography: Elgin Lessley, George Peters
Edited by: Herbert Warren
Production company: Comique Films
Distributed by: Paramount Pictures

Not one, but two bell boys – in the form of Fatty and Buster – are wreaking their customary havoc in the lobby of Ouchgosh's low-rent Elk's Head Hotel, which comes complete with horse-powered elevator. When Cutie Cuticle arrives at the hotel, the bell boys are awe-struck. Fatty persuades Buster and the desk clerk to fake a robbery at the bank next door, enabling Fatty to show Cutie his heroic side. But they arrive to find that the bank is being robbed for real.

Mindful of Joe Keaton's low opinion of the movie-making business, *Variety* asked him how he felt about appearing in *The Bell Boy*. "Oh it's all right if Arbuckle wouldn't try and tell me how to kick my boy. Shucks [or its equivalent], ain't I been kicking him all his life?"

The film comes to a natural conclusion after 18 minutes with Fatty having got his girl, but there then follows the eight-minute bank robbing scene designed to make Cutie see what a hero Fatty is. Which seems a bit superfluous, plot-wise.

Towards the end of the film, there is a long shot of the driver of a horsecar leaping onto the horse when the straps break to the carriage and the horse makes a run for it. The first time it was filmed, the driver missed the horse's back. Understandably wary of giving it another go, it fell to Buster to do the stunt. Being novices in the horse department, they didn't realise that horses can see behind them, and so the horse once again sidestepped as Buster leapt onto its back and bolted ahead, dragging Buster in its wake. The sequence is over in a second and easily missed, but clearly Roscoe and Buster felt it worth the effort.

Elgin Lessley joins the team as cameraman for the first time. He would be with Buster on 30 films. He quickly became indispensable to Buster, supremely capable in his art, and with the imagination and technical know-how to allow Buster to push back the boundaries of possibility offered by the humble hand-cranked camera.

In April the Balboa Amusement Producing Company Studios at Alamitos Avenue and Sixth Street in Long Beach, California were renamed the Comique Film Corporation Studios.

Roscoe and Buster with Charles Dudley

Moonshine

Directed by: Roscoe "Fatty" Arbuckle
Produced by: Joseph M. Schenck
Presented by: Joseph M. Schenck
Written by: Roscoe "Fatty" Arbuckle
Released: 13 May 1918
Length: 23 minutes (2 reels)

Cast:
Roscoe "Fatty" Arbuckle – Revenue captain
Buster Keaton – Revenue lieutenant
Al St. John – Mountain man and suitor
Charles Dudley – Jud Grew, moonshiner
Alice Lake – Moonshiner's daughter
Joe Bordeaux

Cinematography: George Peters
Edited by: Herbert Warren, Buster Keaton
Production company: Comique Films
Distributed by: Paramount Pictures

> Fatty and Buster are two revenue agents hunting down bootleggers in the Virginia hills. Fatty encounters the daughter of the chief bootlegger and an improbably rapid romance ensues. The bootleggers then capture the two agents, but Buster escapes. Having also escaped thanks to a ruse he happens to have read in *The Count of Monte Cristo*, Fatty rejoins Buster who picks off the bootleggers one by one. Only the leader remains, who gives his blessing to his daughter's romance, Fatty having proven his worth.

There is currently no good quality – i.e. 35 mm – print of the entire film, only around six minutes are held by the Cineteca Nazionale in Rome. A greatly inferior quality 16 mm reduction positive exists in the public domain.

There is an intriguing sequence in which Roscoe calls for reinforcements and Buster opens a car door to allow (by my count) 50 agents to get out. The sequence is one continuous long shot, and so all 50 men seem to emerge from the car. This is clearly done by masking off the left-hand side of the camera lens so that the actors can't be seen getting into the car from that side, and then rewinding the film, masking off the right-hand side and reshooting just the left-hand side with no actors involved. But knowing that, even today the effect

The
reinforcement

is arresting. An interesting background to this is that Buster realised that the effect could be sabotaged by the car's suspension – the car would bob up and down slightly on the side where the actors were climbing out while the other side of the car remained resolutely static. To avoid this, the car was invisibly propped up on blocks so that it remained rock solid throughout, and the effect is realised perfectly.

The film gives the first outing of Buster's remarkable ape impersonation, which he would elaborate on for *The Playhouse*. It takes place in the context of an impressive chase scene with Al St. John, also displaying simian symptoms. The sequence is brilliant and hilarious, but somewhat undermined by the fact that we have absolutely no clue as to why they should start to behave like apes in the first place.

Moonshine is notably post-modern in that the dialogue references filmic traditions, although refreshingly so and never to the point of being irritating:

> "This is absurd! You abuse my daughter and she embraces you!" / "Our film is only a two-reel short. No time for preliminary love scenes!" / "In that case, go on … I don't care. I don't want to ruin your masterpiece."

> "Where are the extras?" / "It's lunch break. I'll just do the same …"

Filming took place in the San Gabriel canyon, just north of Los Angeles. Press reports at the time suggest the shoot was beset by flood water raging through the canyons, marooning the crew in the mountains for ten days.

Good Night, Nurse!

Directed by: Roscoe "Fatty" Arbuckle
Produced by: Joseph M. Schenck
Presented by: Joseph M. Schenck
Written by: Roscoe "Fatty" Arbuckle
Released: 8 July 1918
Length: 20 minutes (2 reels)

Cast:
Roscoe "Fatty" Arbuckle – Fatty
Buster Keaton – Woman with umbrella / Dr. Hampton
Al St. John – Man in bandages / Surgeon's assistant
Alice Lake – Crazed woman
Alice Mann – Inmate
Joe Keaton – Assistant
Kate Price – Nurse
Dan Albert – Butler / Hospital orderly
Snitz Edwards – Drunken man
Joe Bordeaux

Cinematography: George Peters
Edited by: Herbert Warren
Production company: Comique Films
Distributed by: Paramount Pictures

Inexplicably standing outside a general store in torrential rain, Fatty is using all his ingenuity in trying to light a cigarette. When he brings home a couple of gypsy musicians and their monkey, his wife decides he should check in to the No Hope Sanitorium. Surgery is required when he accidentally eats a thermometer and he is put under using quantities of ether. Having helped a patient to escape, he finds himself back in the hospital. He dons the uniform of a suitably well-proportioned nurse, but before he can make his second escape, Doctor Buster Hampton appears and is rather smitten. Some slightly uncomfortable flirting ensues, naturally ending in slapstick. Fatty makes a break for it, but ends up joining – and winning – a race for men weighing over 200 pounds. The sanatorium staff catch up with him and wrestle him to the ground … at which point he awakens from his ether-induced surgery.

The sanatorium used in the film is the Arrowhead Hot Springs Hotel near San Bernadino, west of Los Angeles.

Snitz Edwards would memorably play key roles in *Seven Chances*, *Battling Butler* and *College*, although his scene in *The General* was cut just before the film's release.

The identity of the man in bandages whom Fatty and his daughter meet when they enter the sanitorium is not obvious. Some sources claim it is Joe Keaton, probably because Fatty is downed by a high kick that is so characteristic of Joe. However, from his skinny build, manic demeanour and toothy grin, we can be pretty certain that this is Al St. John.

The Cook

Directed by: Roscoe "Fatty" Arbuckle
Produced by: Joseph M. Schenck
Presented by: Joseph M. Schenck
Written by: Roscoe "Fatty" Arbuckle
Released: 15 September 1918
Length: 21 minutes (2 reels)

Cast:
Roscoe "Fatty" Arbuckle – Chef
Buster Keaton – Assistant chef
Al St. John – Holdup man
Alice Lake – Waitress / Cashier
Glen Cavender – Diner
Luke – The dog

Cinematography: George Peters
Edited by: Herbert Warren
Production company: Comique Films
Distributed by: Paramount Pictures

With Fatty in the kitchen and Buster waiting tables, service at the Bull Pup Cafe is inevitably unconventional. The juggling and acrobatics are non-stop until the unexpected appearance of an exotic dancer in the middle of the dining room divert the pair, who then add their own brand of Eastern dance to the mix. Act two plays out by the beach with Buster on a date at the fair with the waitress and Fatty spending a less-than-relaxing afternoon on a fishing trip with Luke the dog.

The film was thought lost until a print was discovered along with *A Reckless Romeo* in the Norwegian Film Archive in 1998. A second print with extra footage was discovered in the Netherlands in 2002. Nevertheless, the last minute or so of the film are missing, so we're not sure how the rescue of waitress Alice Lake pans out. The DVD released by Milestone Films in 2003 includes a final title card that is based on the original press kit:

> "While the pest waiter is rescuing his girl with the aid of the cook, the courageous Luke dives into the ocean after the tough guy, chasing him so far out in to the ocean that he can't swim back to shore. It is fitting that after all this action, everything ends happily."

The release date was put back from 18 August to 15 September.

The Cook was the last film Buster made before joining Company C of the 159th Infantry, 40th Division in July and being sent to France for the final months of the First World War. And after 11 films together, it was also his last film with Alice Lake – or at least his last credited film, as they both are in *A Desert Hero*. Understandably feeling restricted by continual slapstick work, she chose to branch out to seek more varied acting opportunities.

Back Stage

Directed by: Roscoe "Fatty" Arbuckle
Produced by: Joseph M. Schenck
Presented by: Joseph M. Schenck
Written by: Jean Havez
Released: 7 September 1919
Length: 21 minutes (2 reels)

Cast:
Roscoe "Fatty" Arbuckle – Stagehand
Buster Keaton – Stagehand
Al St. John – Stagehand
Charles A. Post – Strongman, Professor Onion
Molly Malone – Strongman's assistant
John Coogan – Eccentric dancer, Clarence Marmalade
William Collier Jr. – Stagehand

Cinematography: Elgin Lessley
Production company: Comique Films
Distributed by: Paramount Pictures

The stagehands are preparing the theatre when the theatrical troupe arrive. Irked by the way that the strongman treats his pretty assistant, the stagehands turn on the troupe, who quit en masse. The show goes on with the stagehands performing, with the strongman's assistant. When the troupe appear in the audience, the fourth wall is well and truly broken.

Released just a year after *The Cook*, this was the first film Buster made after his return from France at the end of the First World War. (To make it clear that he had been nowhere near the front line, he would declare that he was "back from the back".) He had spent two months in hospital in New York being treated for a serious ear infection that he had picked up in France and which had rendered him half deaf. It was a condition from which he never fully recovered, although he would disguise it with a charm that would avoid embarrassing others, as can be seen in his appearance on "This Is Your Life" in April 1957, for example.

Before filming *Back Stage* he undertook a little light stunt work on Roscoe's latest picture, *A Desert Hero*. Suitably padded, Buster doubled for Roscoe tumbling off a freight train, down an embankment, across a street and into a saloon, and, with rather less padding, for Alice Lake who is lassoed onto the back of a horse by Al St. John who then gallops off with her.

The film marks the first appearance of the falling wall gag, which was to feature so spectacularly in *Steamboat Bill, Jr.* Here it is Roscoe who escapes being hit by a falling stage flat by being positioned beneath the upper floor window.

And Fatty's hurling of Buster at an audience member recreates a feature of The Three Keatons' act.

Buster's "Princess Rajah" snake dance routine was presumably as featured in the missing *A Country Hero*, and was something he further developed while in the army in France to entertain the troops. He would use it again for his spot in *The Hollywood Revue of 1929*.

Back Stage was the first of two of Buster's films to feature John Coogan (aka John Henry Coogan Jr.). Coogan brought his son to the shooting of the film, who would entertain the cast between scenes. Two years later, young Jackie Coogan would star alongside Charlie Chaplin in *The Kid*. Buster would look back on *Back Stage* with a modicum of regret at having featured the eccentric Coogan senior, and not recognised the goldmine that was Coogan junior.

William Collier Jr.'s nickname was also Buster. He was born Charles F. Gall, and after his parents divorced, his mother married William Collier Sr. His new father, who would later appear as himself in *Free and Easy*, adopted him and named the boy after himself.

The Hayseed

Directed by: Roscoe "Fatty" Arbuckle
Produced by: Joseph M. Schenck
Presented by: Joseph M. Schenck
Written by: Jean Havez
Released: 26 October 1919
Length: 22 minutes (2 reels)

Cast:
Roscoe "Fatty" Arbuckle – Mailman
Buster Keaton – General store worker
Daniel Crimmins – General store owner
Molly Malone – Fanny
John Coogan – Sheriff
Luke – The dog

Cinematography: Elgin Lessley
Production company: Comique Films
Distributed by: Paramount Pictures

Buster works at the Grimes General Store ("Don't go to the city to be cheated – buy here"), and Fatty is the mailman. While Fatty is delivering letters, the local sheriff, Fatty's rival for the hand of his sweetheart Fanny, sneaks into the store and steals $300 from a registered letter. Buster sees him but is blackmailed into silence. The sheriff buys Fanny an expensive ring but is trumped by Fatty who presents her with a more expensive looking imitation. At an English dance that evening he accuses Fatty of stealing the $300, but Buster exposes him as the true thief. Luke the dog runs the sheriff out of town, clearing Fatty's way to Fanny's heart.

Fanny is called Molly in some prints of the film – no doubt due to the actress being Molly Malone.

This is the first Arbuckle–Keaton short without Roscoe's nephew Al St. John, who had branched out on his own to direct and star in shorts for Sunshine Comedies. Nearly all of these are now lost. He would eventually notch up appearances in around 350 films.

In 1935, John Coogan was killed in a car crash, although his son Jackie survived. John had carefully managed the millions that Jackie had earned as a child star, but by the time the boy was 21, soon after John's death, his mother and step-father had squandered the lot. As a result, a law was passed in California in 1939 – Coogan's Law – to prevent the same happening to other child actors.

Oddly, in the filmography in Rudi Blesh's biography *Keaton*, *The Hayseed* is not listed, but *A Desert Hero* is.

The Garage

Aka *Fire Chief*

Directed by: Roscoe "Fatty" Arbuckle
Produced by: Joseph M. Schenck
Presented by: Joseph M. Schenck
Written by: Jean Havez
Released: 11 January 1920
Length: 22 minutes (2 reels)

Cast:
Roscoe "Fatty" Arbuckle – Mechanic / Fireman
Buster Keaton – Mechanic / Fireman
Molly Malone – Garage owner's daughter

Harry McCoy – Jim, the village heart-throb
Monty Banks – Man with dog
Daniel Crimmins – Rube, the garage owner
Charles Dorety – Car owner
Polly Moran – Shocked woman
Luke – The dog
Alice Lake (unconfirmed)

Cinematography: Elgin Lessley
Production company: Comique Films
Distributed by: Paramount Pictures

> An eventful day at the garage-slash-fire station. Mechanics-slash-firemen Fatty and Buster manage to ward off Jim, the village heart-throb, who is starting to get on the nerves of the owner's daughter, although to be fair the last straw is when she, the suitor and the flowers he brought are doused in oil thanks to the hapless mechanics. Jim gets his own back by sounding a false fire alarm to get rid of Fatty and Buster, but the plan literally backfires and he finds himself trapped in the burning garage.

The stunts include Fatty polishing a car window that turns out not be there, as Buster himself did in *The Bell Boy*, as well as the brief and unexplained appearance of a custard pie.

Alice Lake is sometimes credited as the lady who faints at the sight of a trouserless Buster, though it is by no means certain that it is her.

The Garage, like *The Hayseed*, was filmed at the Thomas Ince studios in Culver City, at the time managed by one Henry Lehrman. Lehrman looms notorious in Roscoe's story.

When he was directing early Keystone Kops films, Lehrman had taken a dislike to Roscoe and tried to get Mack Sennett to fire him. Years later, Lehrman happened to be having an affair with actress Virginia Rappe (no accent on the e, but pronounced Rap-*pay*) when she died following Roscoe's Labor Day party in 1921 (see *Cops*, p. 61, for more information on this tragic episode). As a result Lehrman became Roscoe's most vicious denouncer, although he had been in New York on the fateful day. In fact, Virginia Rappe was pregnant with Lehrman's child at the time and had been at the party to ask Roscoe for money for an abortion, not wanting Lehrman to find out about the pregnancy.

A few days after Rappe's death, Lehrman had obviously managed to get over his grief to the extent that he was able to meet his brand new girlfriend in Manhattan and buy her an expensive fur coat, a fact that only came to light after Roscoe had been acquitted because Lehrman had baulked at paying the bill for the coat.

On 2 April 1920, *Variety* reported that Roscoe, by arrangement with Joseph Schenck, would begin production of a series of five-reel comedies, starting on 12 April. Buster would feature in two-reelers released through Metro from 1 May. Roscoe's first feature was *The Round-Up*, actually a seven-reeler, released on 10 October.

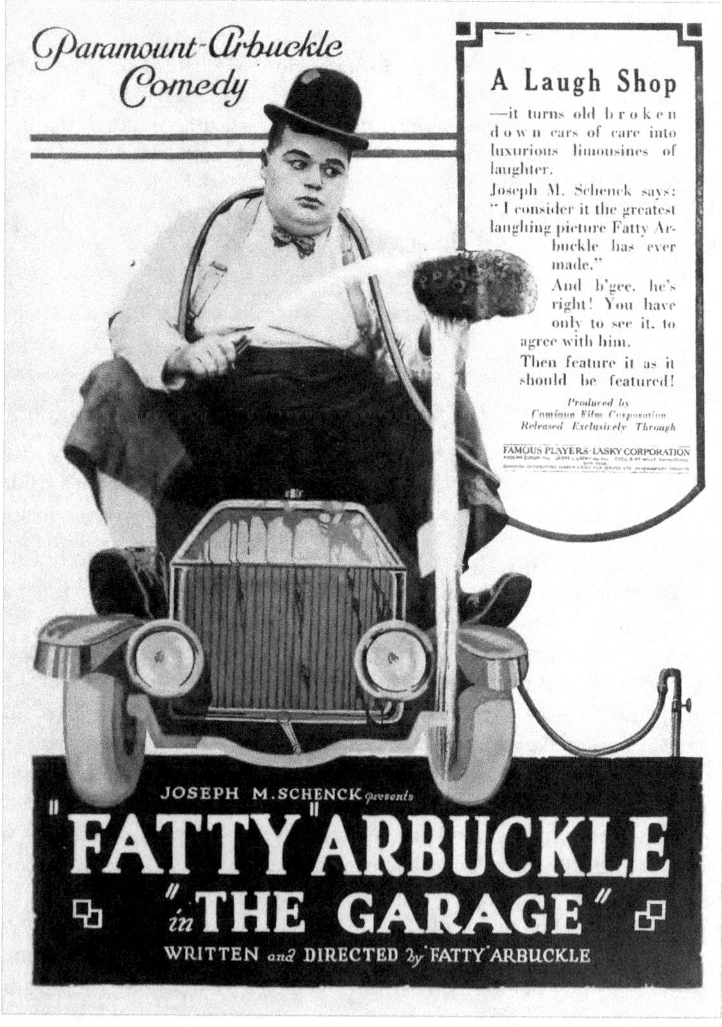

Enter ~ BUSTER KEATON

Here is the comedy sensation of the year, introducing a new stellar comedian, who is going to reach the peaks of funmaking. Buster Keaton has graduated from vaudeville ~ where for years he was a member of the famous **THREE KEATONS** Fatty Arbuckle has nominated this nimble and talented young man as his legitimate successor in the field of short comedy subjects...That's what he thinks of BUSTER

HIS FIRST SIDE-SPLITTING COMEDY ~ PRESENTED BY JOSEPH M. SCHENCK
Written and Directed by BUSTER himself and EDDIE CLINE ~ is

ONE WEEK

which starts him on his larger career. He begins where other comedians left off. He has packed his first two-reel subject with a bundle of brand new "gags" that will set your patrons laughing until (if they wear 'em) their false teeth will drop out and their waist-bands will "shimmy".

METRO

Directed by: Buster Keaton, Edward F. Cline
Produced by: Joseph M. Schenck
Presented by: Joseph M. Schenck
Written by: Buster Keaton, Edward F. Cline
Released: 1 September 1920
Length: 22 minutes (2 reels)

Cast:
Buster Keaton – The groom
Sybil Seely – The bride
Joe Roberts – Piano mover

Photographed by: Elgin Lessley
Edited by: Buster Keaton
Production company: Comique Films
Distributed by: Metro Pictures

The happy couple's wedding present from Uncle Mike is a build-it-yourself house on lot number 99. Having beaten off his rival, Handy Hank, for the hand of his bride, Buster embarks upon building the kit homestead. But Handy Hank has switched the building instruction labels so the house when complete is the darn'dest thing you ever saw, with roof, porch, windows and doors going off at every angle. At the end of the week, after the house has been furnished, and subject to a riotous house warming party and mini hurricane, what remains of it is found to be on the wrong lot and needs to be moved to the other side of the tracks. Cue one of Buster's best and most delightfully executed stunts that brilliantly second guesses his audience.

Comique's deal with Metro gave them 70 per cent of the box office receipts, and gave Buster $1,000 per film plus 25 or 35 per cent of Comique's takings (sources differ). Buster's Metro shorts were to be supervised by his old vaudeville friend Lou Anger, who was Comique's production manager, and who had been key to Buster's first meeting with Roscoe Arbuckle.

The plan was for Buster's solo career to kick off with *The "High Sign"*. But having filmed and edited it, he felt it wasn't strong enough for a debut film.

To help come up with a fresh idea, Buster headed out to Sierra Nevada. Roscoe Arbuckle was there filming his first feature, *The Round-Up*, and Buster naturally took an uncredited role as an American Indian. Before he could come up with an alternative for his own debut however, Metro had cast him in his own feature, *The Saphead*. Buster's parents happened to see *The Round-Up* in their home town in Michigan, as they liked Roscoe, although they were unaware that Buster was in it. As soon as the Native died on screen, Myra said, "That was Buster." Just from the long shot of the Native running. "Nobody else could do that. That body action …"

Buster repeats the gag of the falling wall that was used in *Back Stage* and that would be so memorable in *Steamboat Bill, Jr.* – but here he ups the ante somewhat. Not only is the wall noticeably more substantial than the theatre set we saw in *Back Stage*, but Buster actually walks into position while the wall is falling. Not as death defying as the *Steamboat Bill, Jr.* incarnation, but casually impressive and again a demonstration of Buster's exquisite timing.

The stunt where Buster falls having stepped through the bathroom door into thin air is one of the few where he badly injured himself, needing alternate hot and cold showers and, such was the state of medical thinking at the time, the application of olive oil and horse liniment to ease his swollen arm and back.

An alternative release date of 7 September is sometimes cited.

Having released his first short, Buster notched up his first feature release …

Keaton Has Big Part in "The New Henrietta"

Buster Keaton, for long identified with screen comedies, has been engaged by Metro to play the important role of Bertie in Metro's all-star production of "The New Henrietta." In this special picturization of Winchell Smith's and Victor Mape's revision of the famous old stage play, "The Henrietta," by Bronson Howard, the all-star ensemble will include also that veteran actor, William H. Crane.

The Saphead

Directed by: Herbert Blaché
Personally supervised by: Winchell Smith
Produced by: John Golden, Winchell Smith, Marcus Loew
Presented by: Marcus Loew
Screenplay by: June Mathis
Based on the play "The New Henrietta" by Victor Mapes, Winchell Smith
Adapted from "The Henrietta" by Bronson Howard
Released: 18 October 1920
Length: 75 minutes (7 reels, 6,650 feet)

Cast:
William H. Crane – Nicholas Van Alstyne
Buster Keaton – Bertie Van Alstyne
Edward Jobson – Reverend Murray Hilton
Beulah Booker – Agnes Gates
Edward Connelly – Mr. Musgrave
Edward Alexander – Watson Flint
Irving Cummings – Mark Turner
Odette Tyler – Mrs. Cornelia Opdyke
Carol Holloway – Rose Turner
Jack Livingston – Dr. George Wainright
Katherine Albert – Hattie (uncredited)
George Berrell – Jim Hardy (uncredited)
Henry Clauss – Valet (uncredited)
Edward F. Cline – Stock Exchange member (uncredited)
Alfred Hollingsworth – Hathaway (uncredited)
Helen Holte – Henrietta Reynolds (uncredited)
Jeffrey Williams – Hutchins (uncredited)

Photographed by: Harold Wenstrom
Production company: Metro Pictures
Distributed by: Metro Pictures

Although not the brightest of sparks, Bertie Van Alstyne is a good man at heart. He hides his saintliness in the mistaken belief that, as he has read in *How To Win The Modern Girl*, the modern girl "prefers sports to saints". He is a disappointment to his father, the wealthy Nick Van Alstyne, who has greater admiration for his son-in-law Mark Turner. Turner for his part has a secret mistress and illegitimate child. When Bertie is on the point of marrying his father's ward, Agnes, Turner receives news that his mistress has died and the child has arrived with incriminating letters. Turner claims the letters are Bertie's, breaking Agnes' heart and causing Nick to disown his son. However, Turner goes a step too far when he tries to cheat his father-in-law out of his riches, reckoning without the naïve ingenuity of his saphead brother-in-law.

Buster had made *The "High Sign"*, his first two-reeler without Roscoe earlier in the year, but was unhappy with the result. While pondering a follow-up, he was whisked off to star in his first feature. Joe Schenck had reckoned that appearing in a feature film would boost publicity for his forthcoming shorts.

The play "The Henrietta" was originally a hit in 1887, as was its adapted Broadway revival "The New Henrietta" in 1913, with William H. Crane and

Douglas Fairbanks. It was first filmed in 1915 as *The Lamb*, with Fairbanks making his film debut reprising his role as the timid son. Buster took on Fairbanks' role, around which the play was rewritten for *The Saphead*.

While Buster was filming *The Saphead* at Metro studios on Romaine Street, Joe Schenck bought Charlie Chaplin's former Lone Star studio just around the corner on Lillian Way and renamed it the "Buster" Keaton Studio. This allowed Buster to ferry back and forth between the studios, starting work on *One Week* during *The Saphead*'s final days of shooting.

William H. Crane, who plays Buster's father, was in the original production of the play in 1887. Almost exclusively a stage actor, he was credited in just four features, of which this was the second.

Carol Holloway's real name was Carol Halloway, although throughout her career she mostly credited herself as Holloway.

The reviews for Buster's first feature performance, for the first time playing a straight comedic role devoid of any slapstick, were positive. Typical was the view of *Variety*. Having declared William H. Crane "a joy", the paper concluded, "As for Buster, a cyclone when called upon, his quiet work in this picture is a revelation."

The American Film Institute's database gives the release date as 20 September, while some sources cite the copyright date, 11 October.

Convict 13

Directed by: Buster Keaton, Edward F. Cline
Produced by: Joseph M. Schenck
Presented by: Joseph M. Schenck
Written by: Buster Keaton, Edward F. Cline
Released: 27 October 1920
Length: 21 minutes (2 reels)

Cast:
Buster Keaton – Golfer turned prisoner, Guard
Sybil Seely – Socialite, Warden's daughter
Joe Roberts – The crazed prisoner
Edward F. Cline – Hangman
Joe Keaton – Prisoner
Harry Keaton – Prison guard
Louise Keaton (unconfirmed)
Myra Keaton (unconfirmed)

Photographed by: Elgin Lessley
Edited by: Buster Keaton
Production company: Comique Films
Distributed by: Metro Pictures

While Buster plays golf with socialite and prison warden's daughter Sybil Seely, a convict escapes from the nearby jail. An unlucky ricochet knocks Buster out, enabling the convict to swap clothes with him and make his escape. The newly costumed Convict 13 manages to outwit the pursuing cops but in doing so inadvertently locks himself in the prison yard. Here he discovers he is next on the list of those to be hanged. The warden's daughter rescues him from this fate after which he manages to swap clothes with a prison guard he accidentally knocks out while breaking rocks. Capture of the ringleader of the latest riot sees golfer turned convict turned prison guard promoted to Assistant Warden. But reckless use of a sledgehammer and a further concussion sees Buster back at square one.

In an interview with *Picture-Play* during the making of *Convict 13*, Buster said that the film was to be called *It's a Cinch*. "But take it from me, the title-writer is a liar. It isn't!"

Buster's mother Myra may make her screen debut as an extra in *Convict 13*. Buster told *Pictures and Picturegoer* in October 1922 how both his parents had visited him on set for the first time, and had been persuaded to take part in filming. Meanwhile *Motion Picture News* also reported that The Three Keatons had reunited and that Myra had donned a prisoner's costume and taken part.

His sister Louise is also reported to be somewhere in the film, possibly as one of the socialites in the golfing party. If so, this is likely to be the only occasion when all five Keatons – Buster, his parents and his siblings – are in the same film.

Certainly, an element of The Three Keatons' vaudeville act crops up towards the end of the film. Buster, surrounded by a throng of convicts, uses a punch-ball tied to a rope to swing around his head and pick off the cons one by one. On stage, years earlier, he had stood on a table and swung a basketball tied to a rope in a similar style to whack his father as he sang to the audience. The practice remained perfect as the first convict to be walloped is none other than Joe Keaton himself – Buster's first swing meticulously removes Joe's hat and his second one floors the old man completely.

Film Daily reported that Buster had broken a rib by being hit by a brick during filming, although Buster does not seem to be involved in the brick-throwing scene in the finished picture.

The Scarecrow

Directed by: Buster Keaton, Edward F. Cline
Produced by: Joseph M. Schenck
Presented by: Joseph M. Schenck
Written by: Buster Keaton, Edward F. Cline
Released: 22 December 1920
Length: 20 minutes (2 reels)

Cast:
Buster Keaton – Farmhand
Joe Roberts – Farmhand
Joe Keaton – Farmer
Sybil Seely – Farmer's daughter
Luke – The "mad" dog
Edward F. Cline – Hit and run truck driver

Photographed by: Elgin Lessley
Edited by: Buster Keaton
Production company: Comique Films
Distributed by: Metro Pictures

Two farmhands share a one-room shack, and a love for the farmer's daughter ("I don't care how she votes – I'm going to marry her"). Technical ingenuity ensures that the shack has all home comforts – the phonograph doubles up as a stove, the bed as a piano, the sofa as a sink, and the table top as a wall plaque: "What Is Home Without a Mother?". Pursued by what he believes to be a mad dog, Buster eventually takes refuge in a threshing machine, which removes his clothes. He is forced to don the clothes of the eponymous scarecrow, but the outsize slap shoes trip him up in front of the farmer's daughter, who assumes his kneeling position is a proposal of marriage. She gladly accepts. Fleeing her father's wrath on a stolen motor bike, the two fortuitously scoop up a passing minister ensuring no time is lost in completing the wedding ceremony.

The dog that pursues Buster is none other than Luke, star of a number of Arbuckle–Keaton shorts. The Staffordshire bull terrier actually belonged to Roscoe's wife Minta Durfee, and appears here for the only time in a film not to feature Arbuckle himself. Luke was reported to be making $200 a week when he was appearing in Mack Sennett films.

Al St. John is sometimes incorrectly credited as the either the motorcycle owner or the priest, but he is neither. Various sources claim that a young Mary Astor also appears, but apart from Sybil Seely, the only actress in the film is the uncredited farmer's wife, who looks old enough to be Mary Astor's grandmother.

Sybil Seely gives Joe Keaton a taste of his own medicine as she floors him with a rather impressive high kick to the head.

Some sources describe the farmhands as brothers.

Buster was to give a brief insight into his slap shoes in the 1965 documentary *Buster Keaton Rides Again*: "They weigh about five pounds each. These shoes are eleven-and-a-half. I wear a seven-and-a-half. So I got a lot of room in here."

Neighbors

Directed by: Buster Keaton, Edward F. Cline
Produced by: Joseph M. Schenck
Presented by: Joseph M. Schenck
Written by: Buster Keaton, Edward F. Cline
Released: 3 January 1921
Length: 18 minutes (2 reels)

Cast:
Buster Keaton – The boy
Virginia Fox – The girl
Joe Roberts – The girl's father
Joe Keaton – The boy's father
Edward F. Cline – The cop
Jack Duffy – The judge
The Flying Escalantes

Photographed by: Elgin Lessley
Edited by: Buster Keaton
Production company: Comique Films
Distributed by: Metro Pictures

The age old Romeo and Juliet story plays out over the fence separating two tenement buildings. After many intensely physical efforts by the respective fathers to keep the star-cross'd lovers apart, the families eventually go to court. Both families are bound over to keep the peace, and the judge orders them not interfere in the couple's wedding plans. Nevertheless, the wedding day descends into more domestic warfare before the ring can be placed on the bride's finger, and the couple sneak off on the shoulders of a couple of acrobatic guests. They somehow tumble from the street into a cellar where they happen to find the judge, who breaks off shovelling coal into a furnace to finally declare them man and wife.

This was Buster's first film with Virginia Fox, who would go on to appear in ten of Buster's shorts. She married producer Darryl F. Zanuck in 1924, and although they separated in 1956, they never divorced.

Neighbors underwent a number of changes in its title before it was finally released – *Film Daily* tried its best to keep track, announcing *Paradise Alley* on 11 September 1920, *The Backyard* two weeks later, and the variation *The Back Yard* the following week. At some stage the title *Mailbox* had also been mooted.

Some sources give the film's release date as 22 December 1920.

Buster atop the Flying Escalantes

The Haunted House

Directed by: Buster Keaton, Edward F. Cline
Produced by: Joseph M. Schenck
Presented by: Joseph M. Schenck
Written by: Buster Keaton, Edward F. Cline
Released: 10 February 1921
Length: 24 minutes (2 reels)

Cast:
Buster Keaton – Bank clerk
Virginia Fox – Bank president's daughter
Joe Roberts – Bank cashier
Edward F. Cline – Customer in bank
Dorothy Cassil – Flirting customer
Mark Hamilton – Tallest ghost
Natalie Talmadge – Fainting customer

Photographed by: Elgin Lessley
Edited by: Buster Keaton
Production company: Comique Films
Distributed by: Metro Pictures

The cashier at the 1st National bank is also a counterfeiter, and has nurtured the reputation that his home is haunted to deflect attention from the counterfeiting that goes on there. But he fears the president of the bank may be on to the counterfeiting scheme and tells his cohorts to stage a hold-up. Meanwhile the bank's less-than-ept clerk accidentally spills glue over a pile of banknotes resulting in chaos. As a consequence, the hold-up is thwarted but the clerk is assumed to be responsible. A series of logical but convoluted events sees the clerk, the police, the counterfeiters, the president and his daughter, together with a local opera troupe in full Faustian regalia, descend on the "haunted" house. With everyone in place, the haunting can commence.

Dorothy Cassil signs her own name on the card that she gives to Buster.

The film was shot in November/December 1920 in the Brunton Studios, which would eventually become the base for Paramount Pictures.

Harold Lloyd had released *Haunted Spooks* some months earlier. It was during filming of this that a prop bomb he was holding exploded, temporarily blinding him and tearing off his right thumb and forefinger. In his subsequent films Lloyd wore a prosthetic glove to hide his missing digits.

Roscoe Arbuckle's March 1921 release, *The Dollar a Year Man*, also featured a haunted house.

Contemporary sources also cite a 21 February release.

Hard Luck

Directed by: Buster Keaton, Edward F. Cline
Produced by: Joseph M. Schenck
Presented by: Joseph M. Schenck
Written by: Buster Keaton, Edward F. Cline
Released: March 1921
Length: 22 minutes (2 reels)

Cast:
Buster Keaton – Suicidal boy
Virginia Fox – Virginia
Joe Roberts – Lizard Lip Luke
Bull Montana – Virginia's husband
Bessie Wong – Chinese wife

Photographed by: Elgin Lessley
Edited by: Buster Keaton
Production company: Comique Films
Distributed by: Metro Pictures

Down on his luck, Buster is constantly thwarted in his attempts to end it all, however his final effort sees him on the hunt for an armadillo for the local zoo. The armadillo hunt becomes a fox hunt, after which Buster finds himself front and centre in a raid on a country club by Lizard Lip Luke's gang. Gaining confidence with every unlikely plot development, Buster finally proposes to the girl, who tells him she is already married. All that remains for him to do is to swan-dive from the country club's high board … missing the pool by about a yard and diving into the depths of the earth. Years later he emerges from the hole in the ground, complete with his Chinese family in tow.

For the final stunt – which of course involves no camera trickery, Buster really does dive from nearly 25 feet up – the pool was partly covered with wax paper to blend in with the deck around the pool. From the high board, Buster couldn't fully make out what was fake deck and what was real. He would later claim that a gust of wind forced him to jump.

This final dive is a rare example of Buster using an "impossible" gag, as opposed to one that was just incredibly unlikely. He would normally frame such impossible scenes in the context of a dream, and certainly would not use them in a feature length film, as he felt it was unfairly suckering the audience. In fact, interviewed by *Picture-Play* in February 1928, he used the gag as an

example of how audiences had changed even in the intervening seven years. "That sequence broke all records for long laughs, but if I did it today, it would die at the first preview."

The film was thought lost until 1987, when a version was discovered and reconstructed by Kevin Brownlow and David Gill with Raymond Rohauer – although it still missed the final gag. That final scene was later discovered in a Russian archive.

However, it's likely that footage is also missing from the beginning of the film, possibly showing how he came to be "fired from his job, jilted by his girl, down on his luck", as the first title card of the currently available version puts it.

The statues among which Buster hides are in Macarthur Park, Los Angeles.

Sources vary as to the release date, giving 11 or 16 March 1921.

The "High Sign"

Directed by: Buster Keaton, Edward F. Cline
Produced by: Joseph M. Schenck
Presented by: Joseph M. Schenck
Written by: Buster Keaton, Edward F. Cline
Released: 12 April 1921
Length: 21 minutes (2 reels)

Cast:
Buster Keaton – Our hero
Bartine Burkett – Miss Nickelnurser
Ingram B. Pickett – Tiny Tim (tall villain)

Charles Dorety – Drunk in shooting gallery
Al St. John – Man in target practice
Joseph M. Schenck – Shotgun man in shooting gallery

Photographed by: Elgin Lessley
Edited by: Buster Keaton
Production company: Comique Films
Distributed by: Metro Pictures

Despite having no shooting experience, when our hero sees a wanted ad for an assistant in a shooting gallery, he decides to give it a go. His technical ingenuity makes up for his lack of firearms skill and he succeeds in impressing his boss. He also impresses wealthy miser August Nickelnurser, who is in need of a bodyguard as he is being threatened by the gang of bandits known as the Blinking Buzzards. Nickelnurser (and his pretty daughter) recruit Buster on the spot. By a marvellous coincidence, the leader of the Blinking Buzzards is none other than the owner of the shooting gallery, who enrols Buster in the gang ("Do you know the nature of an oath?" "Yes, I play golf"). His first task is to kill the very man he is meant to be protecting.

Although *The "High Sign"* was the first short that Buster filmed for Joe Schenck in early 1920 after his split with Arbuckle, he didn't feel it was strong enough to launch his solo career and insisted it was shelved. It finally got a release when he was out of action for several weeks having broken his ankle filming *The Electric House*.

Bemused by Buster's sharpshooting practice on the beach is Al St. John, making his last appearance with Buster in a short until 1937. He had appeared in all but the last two of the fifteen Arbuckle–Keaton shorts, and so would have been a shoe-in for Buster's first solo venture.

Blinking Buzzards leader Ingram B. Pickett was seven feet tall. He later stood for political office in New Mexico with the slogan "Big enough to serve you, small enough to need you".

Walking towards a discarded banana skin, Buster cheats the audience by not slipping on it, flashing them a quick "high sign" as he walks out of shot. In *My Wonderful World of Slapstick*, Buster writes that he realised that outsmarting the audience in this way and (literally) thumbing his nose at them was a mistake, and added a shot in which he slipped on a second banana skin. However, if this was the case the scene does not appear in surviving prints of the film.

Bartine Burkett appeared in over 50 films before retiring when she married Ralph Zane in 1928. After his death 40 years later, she came out of retirement for a number of film and TV roles. Her last appearance was in 1984 at the age of 86.

The Goat

Directed by: Buster Keaton, Mal St. Clair
Produced by: Joseph M. Schenck
Presented by: Joseph M. Schenck
Written by: Buster Keaton, Mal St. Clair
Released: 18 May 1921
Length: 23 minutes (2 reels)

Cast:
Buster Keaton – The scapegoat
Virginia Fox – Chief's daughter
Joe Roberts – Police Chief
Mal St. Clair – Dead Shot Dan (unconfirmed)
Edward F. Cline – Cop by telephone pole
Jean Havez – Cop cleaning gun
Kitty Bradbury (unconfirmed)

Photographed by: Elgin Lessley
Edited by: Buster Keaton
Production company: Comique Films
Distributed by: Metro Pictures

Dead Shot Dan is having his mug shot taken, but quick thinking on Dan's part ensures not only is it Buster's face that is photographed, but also that he makes his escape. Blissfully unaware, Buster enjoys what we assume is a typical day in which he is relentless pursued by a police posse, pausing only to come to the rescue of a pretty girl. He escapes to the next town, by which time news of Dead Shot Dan's escape, complete with the mug shot of Buster, has reached newspapers and billboards. Once again circumstances see him on the run from the police, this time in the form of its ample framed chief, when he runs into the girl, who in gratitude for his earlier gallantry invites him back for tea. More deft evasion by Buster is called for when her father arrives home and is none other than the police chief. The apartment block elevator features prominently in the ensuing chase.

When Buster rides into the new town, he does so seated on the front of a locomotive in an iconic scene where the train steams in from the distance and stops dead, right in front of the camera, so that the seated Buster fills the frame. This simple but beautifully elegant shot was clearly the result of clever coordination using the remarkable timing skills of cameraman Elgin Lessley (see "Twenty-Five Busters and Other Marvels", p. 55). The train appears to approach us at a pretty constant rate before stopping short in close up. We then have a few seconds of Buster calmly contemplating his arrival. But of course a steam train takes a considerable time to slow down and stop, and so Lessley must have gradually undercranked the film in time with the slowing down of the train, and then reverted to normal speed when the locomotive actually stopped. When played at the correct speed, the gradual slowing of the train is counteracted by the increase in speed due to the undercranking, and so it seems to travel at a constant speed, until it comes to a sudden – but very natural – halt.

What is all the more impressive, though less obvious, is that when the camera is cranked more slowly, more light falls onto the film, and this would need to be compensated for to avoid overexposing the film.

The role of Dead Shot Dan is reported to be taken by Mal St. Clair, although the actor playing the part is maybe both too short and too old to be the director.

Some sources credit Joe, Myra and Louise Keaton as appearing in the film, although this is nigh on impossible to confirm.

Buster's last Metro film was his sixth short release in six months.

The Playhouse

Directed by: Buster Keaton, Edward F. Cline
Produced by: Joseph M. Schenck
Presented by: Joseph M. Schenck
Written by: Buster Keaton, Edward F. Cline
Released: 6 October 1921
Length: 23 minutes (2 reels, 1,803 feet)

Cast:
Buster Keaton – Audience/orchestra/minstrels/interlocutor/dancers/stagehand
Edward F. Cline – Orangutan trainer
Virginia Fox – Twin
Joe Roberts – Actor–stage manager
Monte Collins – Civil war veteran
Joe Murphy – One of the Zouaves
Jess Weldon – One of the Zouaves
Ford West – Stagehand

Photographed by: Elgin Lessley
Edited by: Buster Keaton
Technical director: Fred Gabourie
Production company: Comique Films
Distributed by: First National Pictures

A vaudeville show is populated by numerous Buster Keatons, with many more making up the audience. It transpires that the whole show is being dreamt by Buster himself, a stagehand at a vaudeville theatre. Having woken, Buster goes to work, and an act arrives consisting of twins, one of which Buster quickly falls for – although he's never 100 per cent sure which one. When he accidentally lets a performing orangutan loose, he has to don ape makeup and play the part himself. He is also behind the theatre's stage manager accidentally walloping another of the acts, causing them to quit, and so recruits a team of roadworkers to play Zouave performing infantrymen. He saves the day when an underwater stunt goes wrong, but succeeds in flooding the theatre and auditorium. Amid the pandemonium, he whisks his girl off to the Justice of the Peace to get married, then dashes back to the theatre to whisk off the correct twin this time, marking her with an "X" to avoid any further confusion.

The poster advertising the show at the opening of the film boasts "25 minstrels", and indeed Buster plays 25 parts in addition to the patron buying the ticket:

a conductor, a violinist, a cellist, a bass player, a clarinettist, a trombonist, a drummer, a stagehand, eight minstrels and an interlocutor, and two dancers, as well as six audience members – a smart couple, an elderly couple, and a schoolboy with his grandmother.

The technique for producing three Buster Keatons on film by carefully masking off the relevant sections of film in the camera was fairly well-known – although by no means an easy thing to do. But to produce a scene with nine Busters required Buster and cameraman Elgin Lessley to devise an entirely new technique, as discussed below in "Twenty-Five Busters and Other Marvels".

"This fellow Keaton seems to be the whole show," Buster remarks to himself having read his own name playing every part in the theatre programme. This may also be a dig at the multi-talented Chaplin, but *The Playhouse* is certainly intended to parody Thomas H. Ince, who produced some 600 films between 1910 and 1924, and was known as the "Father of the Western". He was notorious for crediting himself in his films, as presenter, producer, director, supervisor, and even makeup supervisor. Ince's studio, located four miles north of Santa Monica, was known as "Inceville". His elder brother John appeared with Buster in *Three on a Limb* and *Grand Slam Opera*.

In 1909, The Three Keatons performed at the Palace Theatre in London on the same bill as a performing monkey called Peter the Great, which could do almost anything its trainer did. Buster obviously remembered the monkey well, modelling his scene as a performing ape on the bike-riding, cigar-smoking, roller-skating, dining table antics of Peter the Great.

After eight two-reelers for Metro, Buster's contract expired and *The Playhouse* was the first of his films for First National Pictures. First National was founded in 1917 by independent theatre owners to challenge the power of the major distribution companies, in particular Paramount and Loew's Inc. Coincidentally, *The Playhouse* was the first project after Buster broke his leg on the first incarnation of *The Electric House*. It's not obvious in the finished film, but Buster's stunts are rather less energetic than usual – the break was still healing and he was under doctor's orders not to go overboard with the physical comedy.

The Playhouse was also the first with Fred Gabourie as technical director. Gabourie quickly became Buster's right-hand man, responsible for set construction and special effects. It was a perfect match as Gabourie was supremely inventive and just the man to put Buster's ideas into practice. The two worked together on all Buster's films up to his first MGM feature, *The Cameraman* in 1928. Gabourie's name, incidentally, is credited as often as not without the final e, and Rudi Blesh's *Keaton* refers to him as Gabouri. He was a member of the Seneca Indian Tribe, which may be why there is inconsistency over the spelling of his name. But as the later credits seem to settle on Gabourie, that's what we'll use.

Twenty-Five Busters and Other Marvels

While the special effects on show in *The Playhouse* are remarkable, it's worth stressing how the (to say the least) limited technology of the time makes these visual effects quite breathtaking.

Back in the 1920s there was naturally no post-production technology, no green screen, and of course nothing like CGI, to achieve visual effects. But what maybe does need saying is that everything had to be done on the film while it was still inside the camera. Editing film could produce dramatic effects, but even a relatively straightforward dissolve or cross-fade from one scene to the next was not a trivial process. To do this, the first scene was shot and at the point of dissolve, the iris of the camera lens was slowly closed. The film was then physically rewound to the point where the dissolve began, that is, where the closing of the iris started, and the next scene was to start to cross-fade in. This following scene was then set up, and filming would start, the closed lens iris gradually opening until fully open and the scene could get underway. Of course, should there be a mistake in that following scene, the dissolve would be useless and filming would have to start again at the beginning of the first scene.

What's also easy to forget is that the film was hand cranked. Of course the cameramen (for they were nearly all men) were skilled at cranking the film at a constant and consistent rate. But they would also need to be consistent in cranking the film *backwards* and be confident that they would start the cross-fade at the correct place on the unseen and undeveloped film. There were no

visual clues on the film, it was a matter of keeping track by either timing or counting the number of turns of the handle – turns that were carried out at a constant, consistent rate.

Having two Busters side by side involved a similar technique, except that to achieve this, half of the lens was taped off, one Buster was shot on the exposed half of the film, then the film rewound, the other half of the lens taped off and the other Buster shot on the unexposed half of the film. While such effects were thrilling for the audience, the techniques were relatively commonplace. Nevertheless, timing was everything. The perfect timing of the interplay between the Busters in the audience in *The Playhouse* is particularly stunning if we remember Buster is playing off a memory of his other performance, while cameraman Elgin Lessley is faithfully cranking at his constant, consistent speed. Even more stunning are the perfectly synchronised dancing Busters. He was helped here by someone playing a banjo to a metronome, but this shouldn't detract from Buster's performance and again the supreme camerawork of Elgin Lessley, whom Buster called the "human metronome".

At the time, this would typically be about as far as multiple imagery would go, but Buster being Buster decided to up the ante by a factor of four-and-a-half. He and Lessley kept the secret of how they achieved nine Buster minstrels side by side to themselves for many years. It was clear to contemporary film-makers that it wasn't feasible to accurately tape off all but one ninth of the lens without overlap problems, and they were baffled as to how such an astounding result was achieved. In fact, Buster and Lessley built a light-proof box, about a foot square, with nine tightly fitting shutters and attached it to the camera. The shutters were opened one at a time to capture each of the nine performances. Buster was typically self-effacing when he explained the process to Rudi Blesh: "it was hardest for Elgin Lessley at the camera. He had to roll the film back eight times, then run it through again. He had to *hand-crank* at *exactly* the same speed *both* ways, *each* time."

Of course, both actor and cameraman had to come up with the goods. A mistake at any stage of filming – by Buster or Lessley – would ruin the entire effect and the process would have to start again from Buster number one. And even then, they wouldn't know for sure if they'd got it right until the film was developed.

And while we're discussing camera effects we can maybe get ahead of ourselves and look at how the technique worked for a couple of effects that are best showcased in *Sherlock Jr*.

In one scene Buster has been caught and is in a shack with wicked Ward Crane. He is about to grab the stolen pearls from Crane's hand and leap head-first through a window, immediately and unforgettably adopting the disguise of an old woman. Far less showy than the gag of donning the woman's dress is the fade beforehand where a shot of the outside of the shack dissolves so that part of the wall disappears and we can see what Buster and Crane are up to inside. The required a combination of the effects mentioned earlier. The shack was filmed from the outside, then a slow dissolve initiated by closing the iris on the lens. The film was rewound, with the camera kept in exactly the same place, to the point where the slow dissolve started. The shack was then dismantled so that interior could be seen, and the new scene dissolved in, that is, the iris of the lens would be opened at the same rate as it was previously closed. The background would remain unchanged, but the wall would appear to fade. All this for what was in the end just five seconds of film. Most of the audience wouldn't have given this a second thought, but there was of course way more to it than met the eye.

But that was relative child's play – as far as special camerawork is concerned, the most ostentatious effect in *Sherlock Jr.* is the start of the dream section, where Buster rises from his own sleeping self, goes into the auditorium and then enters into the action taking place on the cinema screen. Again it's easy to forget all the effects take place on the film inside the camera. Initially the set was specially brightly lit to make it appear as if the on-screen area was a projected film, but in reality it was simply part of the set that Buster walks into. Having been thrown out of the film (and with a clever cut to sleeping Buster reacting to the fall to mask the change) we enter the sequence of changing on-screen scenes putting Buster in a street, snow, the sea, lions' den, etc. etc. The first couple of changes were relatively straightforward as the "screen" area is a set that is lit to look like a projected movie. The steps outside the house and the garden at night are both filmed as normal, with a cut when Buster is in the same position for the transition. What follows is more involved. The part of the lens corresponding to the cinema screen was taped off and the surroundings (the orchestra and the organist) were filmed for a few minutes, to last throughout the sequence. The film was then rewound and each of the subsequent scenes were filmed separately. The next scene is an exterior street scene and so the camera was set up by the roadside and Buster carefully positioned to correspond with his previous position at the point of the scene change, and at exactly the same distance from the camera, then filming would start.

Buster revealed to Kevin Brownlow how they matched his position so precisely: having done the shot, they would take the film to the darkroom and develop it right there and then. The cameraman would then cut out a frame and put it in the camera gate so he could get Buster in just the right position before starting to film the next section. In fact, a second camera was presumably used for this, positioned alongside the main camera, because as mentioned, the film has no noticeable edits.

Buster then falls backwards into the street, and then jumps to avoid the traffic and pedestrians. At which point Elgin Lessley would stop cranking, everybody would go to the next location, a cliff top, and again the camera set up so that Buster matched his position from the street scene, and then as Lessley starts cranking he instantly stops himself walking into the ravine that has suddenly appeared. And so on through a further five scene changes, with none of the individual scenes lasting more than twenty seconds.

The Boat

Directed by: Buster Keaton, Edward F. Cline
Produced by: Joseph M. Schenck
Presented by: Joseph M. Schenck
Written by: Buster Keaton, Edward F. Cline
Released: 10 November 1921
Length: 23 minutes (2 reels, 2,042 feet)

Cast:
Buster Keaton – The boat builder
Sybil Seely – His wife
Edward F. Cline – SOS receiver

Photographed by: Elgin Lessley
Edited by: Buster Keaton
Technical director: Fred Gabourie

Production company: Comique Films
Distributed by: First National Pictures

> To the despair of his wife, and the mocking indifference of his two pork-pie-hat-wearing children, Buster is building a boat in his garage, which he names the *Damfino*. He overcomes the minor inconvenience of the completed *Damfino* being too big to fit through the garage doors by using brute force to drag the boat through the gap resulting in the partial, and then total collapse of the house. The eventual launch sees the boat glide down the ramp straight to the bottom of the harbour. Having rescued the boat, Buster and his family embark upon an ocean voyage that sees them, and this most unseaworthy of vessels, tested to the limit. They ultimately find themselves in a bathtub, acting as a lifeboat, until, as *Sight and Sound*'s Pauline Houston neatly puts it, "the younger boy, a true Keaton child if ever there was one, very gleefully pulls out the plug."

In 1964, Buster told Kevin Brownlow that it took three days to shoot the ill-fated launch of the boat as it refused to simply glide to the bottom of the river. Attempts using weights and a cut-away stern failed to give the desired effect, so they resorted to dropping an anchor with a cable attached and physically hauled the thing to the bottom of the river. When the scene was recreated for *The Buster Keaton Story* in 1957, Buster's inside knowledge saved Paramount a great deal of time and money.

Buster saw *The Boat* as a continuation of *One Week* – he built the house, now he builds the boat – and so cast Sybil Seely once again as his wife.

The film ends with the family washed up on a beach. "Where are we?" asks Sybil Seely. Buster's mouthed reply, "Damfino", doesn't need a title card. However, the punning nature of the name of the boat obviously caused more genteel patrons to get hot under the collar. It appears on a title card earlier in the film when Buster sends out an SOS and is asked who he is. "Neither do I", telegraphs the coastguard in reply and gets back to his paper. To avoid offending sensibilities, *Moving Picture Age* would give regular advice to exhibitors of cuts to films that should be made "in order that the films may be wholesome for children and young people ... to save otherwise splendid, wholesome pictures from rejection". The June 1922 issue recommended "In Reel 2 cut subtitle 'Damfino'."

Buster was filming *The Boat* when Roscoe Arbuckle invited him to San Francisco over the Labor Day holiday to celebrate having completed three feature films. Buster declined the invitation to the fateful weekend's festivities, and thereby unwittingly avoided involvement in the scandal that destroyed Roscoe's career (see p. 61).

The Paleface

Directed by: Buster Keaton, Edward F. Cline
Produced by: Joseph M. Schenck
Presented by: Joseph M. Schenck
Written by: Buster Keaton, Edward F. Cline
Released: 16 January 1922
Length: 23 minutes (2 reels, 1,935/1,960 feet)
  (Alternative lengths for this and subsequent shorts are taken from the
  bi-monthly publication *The Associated First National Franchise*)

Cast:
Buster Keaton – Little Chief Paleface
Virginia Fox – Native maiden
Joe Roberts – The Native chief

Photographed by: Elgin Lessley
Edited by: Buster Keaton
Technical director: Fred Gabourie
Production company: Comique Films
Distributed by: First National Pictures

Crooked oil sharks steal the lease to American Indians' land, and give them 24 hours to leave. On hearing the news, the Native Chief orders that the next white man to enter the encampment should killed. All eyes turn to the gate, which swings open and in wanders Buster, butterfly net in hand, looking to add to his lepidopteran collection. Initially blissfully unaware of his fate – to the extent that he joins in with the war dance that the Natives are performing prior to despatching him – the penny finally drops and he manages to escape. As luck would have it, he finds asbestos fabric in a hut and fashions himself a suit, which enables him to survive being burnt at the stake upon his recapture, to the astonishment of the tribe. As a result he is dubbed Little Chief Paleface.

With Buster on their side, the Natives set about turning the tables on the oil sharks.

The film is notable as, certainly to start with, it has a much more serious tone that the previous shorts. We see Buster starting to delay the onset of the gags in order to pace the film and give the humour a natural arc. The establishing narrative is relatively extensive and means the first gag, Buster's appearance with a butterfly net, is a full three minutes into the film. Also unusual for the time, the American Indians are portrayed neither as a joke nor as the enemy – and indeed, with the notable exception of chief Joe Roberts, many seem to be played by Native Americans – and they clearly have a genuine grievance.

In one of his most spectacular but overlooked stunts, Buster jumps 85 feet from a suspension bridge into an off-camera net.

The film was shot at the Iverson Movie Ranch in Chatsworth, north-west of Los Angeles. It was a popular location for filming westerns and other rural scenes at the time.

The copyright date for the film was 17 December 1921, and some sources give this as the release date.

Cops

Directed by: Buster Keaton, Edward F. Cline
Produced by: Joseph M. Schenck
Presented by: Joseph M. Schenck
Written by: Buster Keaton, Edward F. Cline
Released: March 1922
Length: 18 minutes (2 reels, 1,725 /1,691 feet)

Cast:
Buster Keaton – The young man
Joe Roberts – Police Chief
Virginia Fox – Mayor's daughter
Edward F. Cline – Hobo
Steve Murphy – Conman selling furniture

Photographed by: Elgin Lessley
Edited by: Buster Keaton
Technical director: Fred Gabourie
Production company: Comique Films
Distributed by: First National Pictures

So, the mayor's daughter won't marry Buster until he proves himself a good businessman. In attempt to demonstrate this, Buster pays a passing conman for a cartload of furniture that unbeknownst to him actually belongs to a family who are in the process of moving house. In a series of unfortunate events involving a rich man's wallet, a goat gland specialist, and terrorist bomb, Buster ends up being pursued by literally hundreds of cops. The mayor's daughter's verdict on his day's work results in a memorably snappy end to one of Buster's most frenetic shorts.

The film's rather unfavourable view of the police is almost certainly connected with the huge scandal that Roscoe Arbuckle was currently embroiled in. On 5 September 1921, he had given a small party at the St. Francis Hotel, San Francisco. During the evening a doctor was summoned to attend to the actress Virginia Rappe, but concluded her symptoms were chiefly down to intoxication. Three days later she died of peritonitis from a ruptured bladder. Roscoe was accused of having raped her with a block of ice and arrested for manslaughter. After two mistrials, notably featuring evidence from so-called witnesses who either had an axe to ground or were not even present at the party, the jury of the third trial unanimously found Roscoe not guilty after just six minutes' deliberation. They also took the highly unusual step of drafting a letter to him, apologising for the injustice of the two earlier trials. Nevertheless, public opinion had already pronounced sentence and, shunned by Hollywood, his career was effectively over. The cynical final shot in *Cops*, which was filmed while Roscoe's trials were in full swing, of a tombstone topped with a porkpie hat was surely Buster's riposte to the appalling injustice that was being meted out to his close friend.

A planned gag had the horse, Onyx, no longer capable of pulling the cart, so that Buster unharnesses him to show him how it is done. At which point he hops up onto the wagon so that Buster ends up pulling the horse. This had to be abandoned when Onyx refused point blank to either climb or be hoisted up onto the wagon. The reason for this became apparent on the following day's shooting – he was a she, and had meantime given birth to a foal. Naturally enough, the foal was christened Onyxpected.

There are no interior scenes in the film – it is the only one of Buster's films to be shot completely outdoors. Silent film location supremo John Bengtson suggests that this may have been by design as at the time the studio was out of action as work was being undertaken to provide a covered stage area.

A variety of dates are given for the film's release. Although some give 16 February, most agree it is later – at the time, *Moving Picture Weekly* listed the release on 11 March.

My Wife's Relations

Directed by: Buster Keaton, Edward F. Cline
Produced by: Joseph M. Schenck
Presented by: Joseph M. Schenck
Written by: Buster Keaton, Edward F. Cline
Released: May 1922
Length: 24 minutes (2 reels, 2,096/2,045 feet)

Cast:
Buster Keaton – The husband
Wallace Beery – Photographer
Monte Collins – The father
Wheezer Dell – Brother
Harry Madison – Brother
Kate Price – Wife
Joe Roberts – Brother
Tom Wilson – Brother
Edward F. Cline – Cop (unconfirmed)

Photographed by: Elgin Lessley
Edited by: Buster Keaton
Technical director: Fred Gabourie
Production company: Comique Films
Distributed by: First National Pictures

> Having accidentally married an irate Irish woman (in circumstances involving an unfortunate postman, a smashed window and a Polish judge who speaks no English), Buster is dragged home to meet his new in-laws. Standing little chance against the big-boned bride's thuggish father and four thuggish brothers, he needs all his wits just to get any food or sleep. But their less-than hospitable attitude to him soon changes when they discover that his late uncle has left him $100,000. Or has he?

It's probably no coincidence that Buster had married into the Talmadge clan, headed by the formidable Peg, a year before making *My Wife's Relations*.

In September 1921, *Photoplay* ran a before-and-after article featuring interviews with single Buster from June 1920 and married Buster from June 1921. The 1920 interview has strong echoes of the marvellous verse in "Makin' Whoopee": "Weddings make a lot of people sad / But if you're not the groom, it's not so bad." Buster says, "Romance, which leads to marriage, begins at home but it finishes in Reno. ... It's a great feeling no doubt to be a member of the ball and chain gang but I prefer to remain single and let the barber massage my head without the aid of a rolling pin." A year later, his altered view was healthily cynical: "I cannot understand a bachelor nor his way of thinking. ... When I was single and returned home I could never find anything to do. Just think of all the things your wife can find for you to do. I have learned in my short married life that there are two sides to every argument – your wife's and her mother's".

The scene of the family at dinner was adapted for *Palooka from Paducah* in 1935, this time with actual Keatons seated around the table.

For many years the film ended rather abruptly with Buster leaping aboard a train bound for Reno. Then an alternative ending was discovered on a diacetate print held by Lobster Films. Here Buster escapes through a third floor window and reaches the pavement by abseiling down the awnings. The *Moving Picture World* review from 6 May 1922 (of "*His Wife's Relations*") confirms the original ending had the escape via the awnings followed by the leap onto the Reno train.

Wheezer Dell was a pitcher for the Vernon Club in the Pacific Coast Baseball League, having previously played for the Brooklyn Dodgers. This was his only acting role – having been cast principally due to his 6'4" frame. Of course being a baseball player also counted in his favour – baseball was very much the leisure pursuit of preference during time out at the Buster Keaton Studios, as is described in "For the Love of Buster" in the introduction to this book. If you skipped it, it really is worth a read.

Some sources give a release date of 12 June.

The Blacksmith

Directed by: Buster Keaton, Mal St. Clair
Produced by: Joseph M. Schenck
Presented by: Joseph M. Schenck
Written by: Buster Keaton, Mal St. Clair
Released: 21 July 1922
Length: 22 minutes (2 reels, 1,764/1,844 feet)

Cast:
Buster Keaton – Blacksmith's assistant
Joe Roberts – Blacksmith
Virginia Fox – Horsewoman

Photographed by: Elgin Lessley
Edited by: Buster Keaton
Technical director: Fred Gabourie

Production company: Comique Films
Distributed by: First National Pictures

> As the result of a violent altercation, the blacksmith is detained at the Sheriff's pleasure and Buster is in charge. An elegant horsewoman leaves her pristine white horse to be shod and Buster helps it select a stylish shoe. Another satisfied customer leaves with a saddle shock absorber designed to make her riding experience less arduous. But the day goes downhill with the inadvertent destruction of a slicker's brand new Rolls Royce and the ire of the owner of the saddle shock absorber which has failed to live up to its promise. When the jail finally proves unable to contain the burly blacksmith, the day's less-than-gruntled clientele join him in turning on Buster.

The story of the film's production is the most convoluted of all Buster's shorts. There had previously been one bit of juggling with Buster's release schedule – *The "High Sign"* had been filmed as Buster's debut short, but was then held back for months until it was needed to fill a gap when he broke an ankle and production of *The Electric House* had had to stop, not being picked up again for nearly a year. But what happened to *The Blacksmith* has for many years been much less clear.

In September 1921 it was reported in *Motion Picture News* and *Exhibitors Herald*, among others, that Buster's latest two-reeler, *The Village Blacksmith*, was complete and being previewed, with advance word that it should be marked as "another button-buster" (which we must assume to be a good thing). Indeed, it was being advertised at the same time as his follow up to *The Playhouse*. But the follow up to *The Playhouse* turned out to be *The Goat*, then came *The Paleface*, and then *Cops*. And after that came *My Wife's Relations*. In May 1922, *Exhibitors Herald* reported that Buster had just completed *The Blacksmith* and *The Frozen North*. *The Blacksmith* was finally released in July 1922.

To add to the confusion, there has long been a bewildering array of slightly and vastly different versions of the film. The hallmark was based on the version discovered by James Mason in the 1950s when he bought Buster's Italian villa and discovered a stack of Buster's films in an outhouse. But copies of *The Blacksmith* held in other collections brought slightly different scenes to the party. Alternative endings show Buster rebuffing the elegant horsewoman's offer of financial recompense for rescuing her from her bolting horse only to have immediate second thoughts, and the other has him slipping a ring off her finger while she is unconscious to then use it to propose to her when she comes round. There are also two different reasons for the horse to bolt. In one it is due to the screams of the woman's mother on seeing oil stains on the horse, unwittingly put there by Buster while on car mechanic duties, and in another an explosion in a manhole frightens the (unstained) horse. At least one version of the film has both scenarios, one after the other.

Then in 2013, film historian Fernando Peña discovered a complete 9.5 mm print of *The Blacksmith* containing about half a reel of completely unfamiliar material. Buster drops on one knee before Virginia Fox, but has barely started his proposal before Joe Roberts lumbers round the corner chasing him off. Finally locking the blacksmith in a shack, Buster manages to propose, only to look up into the face of his intended's father. A little later a 35 mm print of this version was discovered, containing an extra scene in which Buster and Joe Roberts momentarily suspend their chase when they spot the silhouette of a woman undressing behind a drawn blind.

Some excellent detective work by silent film expert John Bengtson has cleared up the confusion. In fact the original version had previewed so badly that Buster had gone back and reshot much of the film. (Buster would later refer to it as "*that* dud".) Bengtson's careful analysis of the various prints, and comparison of the buildings in the far distance of various scenes enabled him to distinguish between the original, rejected 1921 version and the reshot – and at the time officially released – 1922 print. The appearance of new buildings in the background of certain exterior shots, evidently constructed in late 1921/ early 1922, confirmed that the James Mason copy was the original version, shot in 1921, and the newly discovered copy was shot later, in the spring of 1922.

This explains the inconsistencies and repetitions in some prints, which certainly contributes to it being unfavourably received by modern audiences. These were not in any complete individual original print – either original or reshot versions – but came about with various restorations of the film whereby archivists tried to piece together sections of what they thought was a single version of the film. One instance is the disappearing grease stains on the white horse, another is the business of repairing a pocket watch being oddly placed between Buster seeing off the shock-absorbing horse rider and wiping his face as she trots away. The Blu-ray Masters of Cinema *Complete Buster Keaton Short Films 1917–1923* has both original and reshot versions in full, beautifully restored.

The film contains a rare misjudgement by Buster of the public's sense of humour. The scene in which the Rolls Royce is gradually destroyed by an absent-minded Buster was met with a particularly hostile silence, as the destruction of a thing such beauty and expense was felt to be in bad taste.

The Frozen North

Directed by: Buster Keaton, Edward F. Cline
Produced by: Joseph M. Schenck
Presented by: Joseph M. Schenck
Written by: Buster Keaton, Edward F. Cline
Released: 28 August 1922
Length: 17 minutes (2 reels, 2,049/2,058 feet)

Cast:
Buster Keaton – The villain
Joe Roberts – The driver
Sybil Seely – Wife (unconfirmed)
Bonnie Hill – The pretty neighbour
Freeman Wood – Her husband
Edward F. Cline – The janitor
Robert Parker

Photographed by: Elgin Lessley
Edited by: Buster Keaton
Technical director: Fred Gabourie
Production company: Buster Keaton Productions
Distributed by: First National Pictures

The last stop on the subway is the snowy wastes of deepest Alaska where Buster, here playing a villainous role, disembarks. His robbing of a saloon comes to an abrupt halt when it becomes clear his gun-toting partner is a cardboard cut-out. Returning home he is mortified to find his wife in the arms of another man. Only after he has shot both dead does he realise he is in the wrong house. He embarks on a series of exploits, defying the law and generally terrorising the opposite sex. His womanising ways finally catch up with him in the form of his own avenging wife and a pistol. At which point the dreamlike quality of the whole production suddenly makes sense.

The film is unusually dark, with Buster playing an anti-hero. It was conceived as a parody of the Western star William S. Hart, who had been publicly unsupportive of Roscoe Arbuckle in his recent manslaughter case. Buster parodies Hart's melodramatic yet wooden acting style and his propensity, particularly in his later films, for using obviously glycerine tears in an attempt to heighten the emotion of his films. To make the parody absolutely clear – although audiences at the time would have been left in no doubt – the cardboard cut-out that Buster uses at the beginning of the film is an image of Hart in classic pose. Buster also appears briefly dressed as Erich von Stroheim's womanising character from the recent release *Foolish Wives*. By all accounts von Stroheim was delighted by the tribute. Hart reputedly didn't speak to Buster for two years.

There is some debate over the presence of Sybil Seely – both wives bear a striking resemblance to her.

The film was the first to be made after Joe Schenck had changed to the name of Comique Productions to Buster Keaton Productions, as much as anything to distance itself from the Arbuckle scandal. The original title of the film was given in April as *Snow Stuff*.

Shooting took place in Truckee, a town in northern California near the Nevada state line, in late winter 1922. Truckee was becoming the go-to location for films requiring a snowy setting. *Variety* of 17 February 1921 reported that as well as Buster, Betty Compson, Edward Carewe and Ruth Roland were making separate films there, and that hotel beds were being occupied in shifts …

It's not clear why *The Frozen North* was held back until August – it was originally scheduled for release in June, ahead of *The Blacksmith*. In fact it may even have been released and temporarily withdrawn, as the Short Subject Releases section of *The Film Daily Year Book 1922–23* lists the film in June and in August.

Comparing the running time of the currently available version of the film with the reported footage, over six minutes seem to have been lost.

The dear old Northwest Mounted Police have occupied the screens for quite a spell now. But leave it to Buster Keaton to show them all up. He introduces a few little improvements into arctic life, including a subway service, in "The Frozen North," his newest. We're going to be in the audience when Buster gets his man

The Electric House

Directed by: Buster Keaton, Edward F. Cline
Produced by: Joseph M. Schenck
Presented by: Joseph M. Schenck
Written by: Buster Keaton, Edward F. Cline
Released: 19 October 1922
Length: 23 minutes (2 reels, 2,231/2,252 feet)

Cast:
Buster Keaton – Buster
Virginia Fox – The Dean's daughter
Joe Roberts – The Dean
Steve Murphy – Botany degree recipient
Laura La Varnie – Guest

Photographed by: Elgin Lessley
Edited by: Buster Keaton
Technical director: Fred Gabourie
Production company: Buster Keaton Productions
Distributed by: First National Pictures

BUSTER KEATON finds something on his shoulder in "The Electric House," his forthcoming First National attraction.

A mix-up in diplomas at a graduation ceremony sees Doctor of Botany Buster taken on as an electrical engineer to electrify a house while the owners are on holiday. On their return Buster demonstrates the duly electrified house – electric staircase, electric library, electric pool table, electrically operated doors and bath, and dinner served on electric train tracks. Everything works out so well that friends are invited the following day to marvel at the electric miracle. The only potential fly in the ointment would be if the real electrical engineer, swindled out of a job and intent on sabotage, were to make an appearance …

The film originally began shooting in February 1921, but production stopped on the second day when the sole of Buster's slapshoe caught in the electric elevator, breaking his ankle and putting him out of action for several weeks. Buster took advantage of the enforced break from filming to marry Natalie Talmadge, while releasing the shelved *The "High Sign"* and the recently completed *Hard Luck* and *The Goat* to satisfy public demand. Reassuringly, *Variety* reported that the company was four releases ahead of schedule and that Buster would be back to work by the time all four films had been issued.

The exterior shots of the house are of Buster's Westmoreland Place home.

Sources, including the Masters of Cinema *The Complete Buster Keaton Short Films 1917–1923* box set, cite Joe and Myra Keaton as playing Buster's parents in the prologue. Indeed, *Moving Picture World* of 19 August 1922 reports that Eddie Cline suggested casting them as such "just for old times sake". However, if the elder Keatons – or indeed Buster's sister Louise – did appear in the original release, even in some kind of prologue (although no contemporary reviews mention a prologue), no trace of them survives in any currently available version.

Like *The Frozen North*, the given length of the released film suggests footage has been lost – 2,250 feet of film would be expected to run for just under 26 minutes. Certainly there are a number of noticeable jumps in the current version, although not enough to make up for the difference in timings. The missing footage may feature a kitten that appears in a number of publicity shots for the film.

Day Dreams

Directed by: Buster Keaton, Edward F. Cline
Produced by: Joseph M. Schenck
Presented by: Joseph M. Schenck
Written by: Buster Keaton, Edward F. Cline, Roscoe "Fatty" Arbuckle (uncredited)
Released: 27 November 1922
Length: 24 minutes (as currently available) (3 reels, 2,493 feet)

Cast:

Buster Keaton – The young man
Renée Adorée – The girl
Edward F. Cline – The theatre director
Joe Keaton – The girl's father
Joe Roberts – The mayor
George Rowe – Stagehand

Photographed by: Elgin Lessley
Edited by: Buster Keaton
Technical director: Fred Gabourie
Production company: Buster Keaton Productions
Distributed by: First National Pictures

To win the hand of his girl, Buster heads off the city and vows to shoot himself if he isn't a success. His letters tell of a series of appointments as a doctor, financier, renowned performer and police advisor, and his sweetheart dreams of his involvement in suitably heroic activities. The truth is he is employed in an animal hospital, as a street cleaner, as a stage extra, and resorts to petty theft. Resigned to failure he returns home to face his fate.

Surviving prints of *Day Dreams* are incomplete – for each letter home, Renée Adorée dreams of what might be, and we then see what actually is. At least two of the dream sequences are missing in the currently available versions of the film, corresponding to as much as five minutes of missing footage. Stills of the missing scenes appear in Eleanor Keaton's *Buster Keaton Remembered*.

Following his acquittal on 12 April, Roscoe Arbuckle, still popular with the film-going public, remained banned from the screen. Earlier in the year, the Motion Picture Producers and Distributors of America had been set up with the express intention of "cleaning up the pictures" after a number of Hollywood scandals. It was led by the ultra-conservative Will Hays, a man with little knowledge of cinema but with an indefatigable belief in his mission – and who at the time happened to be mixed up in a little financial scandal of his own involving fraudulent transactions by the Republican party campaign. Despite Roscoe's acquittal, pleas from press, public and professionals to allow him to return to work fell on deaf ears. Nevertheless, Roscoe had a staunch friend in Buster. Unable to act or direct, Roscoe resorted to writing, hence his work on *Day Dreams*, which is based on a story he wrote for Buster under the title "The Vision". According to Renée Adorée, Roscoe also directed some of the scenes.

The sequence where the police follow his every step – not because he is advising them but because he is being chased by them – was mostly filmed in San Francisco. Most of the trolley car footage (though confusingly, not all of it) was filmed along Powell Street, which happens to be the street on which the St. Francis hotel stands – the scene of Roscoe's notorious party. No existing *Day Dreams* footage shows the hotel.

Many filmographies give the release of *Day Dreams* as September 1922, ahead of *The Electric House* in October. The original Masters of Cinema *The Complete Buster Keaton Short Films 1917–1923*, for example, puts *Day Dreams* chronologically between *The Frozen North* and *The Electric House*. However, it's clear from contemporary listings that *Day Dreams* was released after *The Electric House*. Both *Motion Picture News* and *Moving Picture World* give the release date for *Day Dreams* as 27 November 1922. *The Film Daily Year Book 1922–23* confirms the date as November 1922. It's true that the film was shot in July and for a short time was announced – in *Film Daily* of 30 June, for example – as Buster's "next comedy". The copyright date of 28 September 1922 may also be the source of the confusion. But the later shorts weren't always released in the order they were filmed – having completed *Day Dreams*, Buster went on to shoot *The Love Nest* at Catalina Island before filming *The Balloonatic* later in the year.

While most reports, notices and advertisements of the time clearly state *Day Dreams* is a two-reeler, it is listed in *Exhibitors Herald* as 2,493 feet. This is long for a two-reel short film, as a single reel is typically around 1,000 feet. The film is occasionally listed (such as in *The Complete Films of Buster Keaton* by Jim Kline) as being a three-reeler, and some contemporary reviews by theatre owners also mention that the film was supplied in three reels ("Three reels of excellent comedy," reports H.J. Longaker of Minnesota, for example). It's likely therefore that the film was called a two-reeler, but was distributed on three reels. One Swedish poster advertised the film as being in three "acts" ("Dagdrömmar – filmfars i 3 akter", namely a film farce in three acts).

The Balloonatic

Directed by: Buster Keaton, Edward F. Cline
Produced by: Joseph M. Schenck
Presented by: Joseph M. Schenck
Written by: Buster Keaton, Edward F. Cline
Released: 22 January 1923
Length: 24 minutes (2 reels, 2,152 feet)

Cast:
Buster Keaton – The young man
Phyllis Haver – The young woman
Babe London – Fat girl at the House of Trouble

Photographed by: Elgin Lessley
Edited by: Buster Keaton
Technical director: Fred Gabourie
Production company: Buster Keaton Productions
Distributed by: First National Pictures

Having emerged from the Tunnel of Love with a black eye, Buster watches disconsolately as the girl he was sitting next to drives off in disgust. He happens upon a hot air balloon launch, but thanks to a faulty basket, the balloon takes off with him in it and the pilot still on the ground. Enough time passes for his black eye to disappear and eventually he is back on terra firma, beside a woodland river. After a spot of unconventional fishing ends in failure, he realises the girl from the Tunnel of Love is relaxing by the same stretch of river. A mishap aboard his boat, the *Minnie-Tee-Hee*, requires her to rescue him, but her disdain for him is undiminished. It takes a bull, a bear and ukulele for him to win her over, their love ultimately defying even gravity …

Shooting finished in October 1923, the last of Buster's silent two-reelers to be filmed.

Buster with
Phyllis Haver –
before and after

The funfair scenes were filmed near Venice Beach, and the rural scenes filmed at the Iverson Movie Ranch in Chatsworth, California, location for shooting *The Paleface*, and to which Buster would return to shoot *Three Ages*.

Babe London, the fat girl who comes hurtling out of the House of Trouble (although a double is clearly used for the stunt), also appears in *Go West*, as the full-figured friend of Roscoe Arbuckle in drag. She is perhaps best known for being the would-be wife of Oliver Hardy in the 1931 Laurel and Hardy short *Our Wife*.

The Love Nest

Directed by: Buster Keaton, Edward F. Cline (uncredited)
Produced by: Joseph M. Schenck
Presented by: Joseph M. Schenck
Written by: Buster Keaton
Released: March 1923
Length: 23 minutes (2 reels, 1,975 feet)

Cast:

Buster Keaton – Buster
Joe Roberts – Captain of the whaler

Virginia Fox – The girl
Steve Murphy – Ship's crew

Photographed by: Elgin Lessley
Edited by: Elgin Lessley
Technical director: Fred Gabourie
Production company: Buster Keaton Productions
Distributed by: First National Pictures

Spurned by his sweetheart, Buster takes to his small boat, the *Cupid*, vowing to sail the seas until he has forgotten her. The presence of her photograph kept constantly next to his heart ensures the chances of this happening are slim. Soon out of gasoline and down to his last biscuit, he chances upon the whaling ship *The Love Nest*. The ruthless captain, who despatches crew overboard for misdemeanours as heinous as spilling coffee, takes to Buster and makes him steward. Buster's ineptness tries the captain to the limit, until the limit is transcended and it's Buster's turn for despatch overboard. Naturally Buster survives, literally hanging on until night time, when he contrives to sink the ship and make off in the lifeboat. He finds himself in the midst of naval target practice, and now surely his luck has run out and only a miracle can save him.

The roster of crew members' names on the clipboard – Charles Frazer, Mack Bullfrog, Frankie Addams, et al. – are supposedly a list of Buster's contemporaries, although this does not seem to be the case. When Buster turns up, Joe Roberts adds the name Frigo to the list – which is one of the nicknames Buster was known by in France.

This was Buster's last film release for First National and his last silent short film (although it was actually shot before *The Balloonatic*). Although he was contracted to make one more two-reeler, the company allowed him to start making feature-length films. He signed with Metro, producers of his first eight two-reelers, on 13 January 1923.

It's the only film that credits both writing and directing solely to Buster.

3 FROM BUSTER KEATON

The 1st — **THREE AGES**

Buster Keaton will make a series of three five-reel super-comedies for Metro, the first of which is *Three Ages*. Each picture in the series will contain all the necessary elements of box-office appeal—story, continuity, direction and photography. Quality of production will be the outstanding mark of every Buster Keaton picture that carries the Metro trade-mark.

The Cast

Wallace Beery   Margaret Leahy
Joe Roberts   Lillian Lawrence
Horace (Cupid) Morgan

Story and Titles by
Jean Havez   Joe Mitchell
and Clyde Bruckman

Directed by
Buster Keaton and Eddie Cline

A Metro Picture

Jury Imperial Pictures Ltd Exclusive Distributors thruout Great Britain Sir William Jury Managing Director . . . .

Directed by: Buster Keaton, Edward F. Cline
Produced by: Joseph M. Schenck
Presented by: Joseph M. Schenck
Written by: Clyde Bruckman, Joseph Mitchell, Jean Havez, Buster Keaton
  (uncredited)
Released: 24 September 1923
Premiere: 25 June 1923, London; 14 July 1923, San Francisco
Length: 63 minutes (6 reels, 5,251 feet)

Cast:
Buster Keaton – The boy
Margaret Leahy – The girl
Wallace Beery – The villain
Joe Roberts – The girl's father
Lillian Lawrence – The girl's mother
Horace Morgan – The Emperor / Cave man / Roman thug (uncredited)
George Davis – Roman guard knocked down (uncredited)
Louise Emmons – Old fortune teller (uncredited)
Blanche Payson – The Amazon (uncredited)
Lionel Belmore (uncredited)
William Norris – Minister (uncredited) (unconfirmed)

Photographed by: Elgin Lessley, William C. McGann
Art director: Fred Gabourie
Production company: Buster Keaton Productions
Distributed by: Metro Pictures

In a parody of D.W. Griffith's silent epic *Intolerance*, the theme of Love is depicted in parallel stories set in the Stone Age, the Roman Age and the Modern Age. Buster competes with his rival for the hand of the dark-haired maiden in a club fight, chariot race and football game.

In 1922, the Schenck/Talmadges put on a contest in England to find a new star to play second lead opposite Norma Talmadge in *Within the Law*. Margaret Leahy beat 80,000 hopefuls to clinch the prize, but, despite being beautiful, was no great shakes as an actress. After three days shooting *Within the Law*, the film's exasperated director told Schenck that either she went or he did. The director stayed, and the actress was palmed off on Buster, who had hoped for Constance Talmadge to play the girl (who incidentally had played the Mountain Girl in *Intolerance*). *Three Ages* would be Margaret Leahy's only film.

Principal filming was completed in March 1923. Normally Buster would test a film with a couple of out-of-town showings to preview audiences. Such was the challenge of getting a credible performance from Margaret Leahy, Buster arranged eight previews of *Three Ages*, reshooting scenes after each one, before he was happy. By the time the film was released, Margaret Leahy had, as *Photoplay* reported at the time, "crept back to England, unnoticed. ... Such is the tragedy of sudden fame." In so doing she hopefully missed *Variety*'s description of her as "the heroine of the Hulton-Talmadge publicity stunt ... who made a distinct screen fiasco opposite Buster Keaton in the picture 'The Three Ages'." The film's London premiere on 25 June was three months before the official release.

This was the first script for Buster credited to Jean Havez since his days with Roscoe. However, Havez had nominally been with Metro since Buster joined – a piece in *Motion Picture News* from 12 June 1920 even stated that he had written *One Week*. Likewise, Clyde Bruckman had been on the team for a while, and had also made uncredited writing contributions to a number of Buster's shorts. It was reported at the time that one Thomas J. Gray had contributed to the script for *Three Ages*, although he isn't credited. The structure of the film – three 20-minute segments set in three distinct periods of history – ensured that were the complete film not to work as a whole, it could be split into three separate two-reelers.

The cavegirl whom Buster tries – unsuccessfully – to drag away by the hair is 6'2" Blanche Payson, who was reputedly San Francisco Police Department's first policewoman. The Stone Age sequence was filmed at Iverson Movie Ranch in Chatsworth, California, some 30 miles north-west of Los Angeles.

Horace Morgan also appears in *Sherlock Jr.* He is normally billed under his professional name of Kewpie Morgan, a corruption of his nickname "Cupid".

The list of football team members is a roll call of cast and crew, including Bruckman, Mitchell, Havez, McGann, Anger and Gabe (Gabourie).

During a rooftop chase, Buster misjudges an 18-foot leap between buildings. This was a genuine error, and he was badly hurt in the fall. He decided to keep the mistake in the film, however, later filming the scramble down the side of the building, through the awnings, swinging on a drainpipe down a pole to end up on the back of a fire engine.

The scene where Buster uses a wooden club as a baseball bat to fell a pursuer with the rock that is thrown at him took between 60 and 76 takes (depending on whose account you read), the knobbly props making the trajectory of the "rock" unpredictable. Nevertheless, Buster wanted to film the sequence in a single take, and not to resort to cutting – caveman throwing rock / cut to: Buster hitting the rock back / cut to: rock hitting caveman in the chest – which he felt would have been cheating. The effort is well worth it, as the brief scene is beautifully smooth and unexpectedly comic.

Buster uses a stand-in for the close up of the shot where he drags off a delighted Stone Age Margaret Leahy. He had lost the tip of his right index finger at the age of three when investigating a clothes wringer belonging to a certain Mrs. Wolgamot, and was aware that this would be seen on screen – although the finger is masked by Ms Leahy's mass of curls.

Just one copy of the film is known to exist, which, although complete, is badly damaged in a number of places.

Buster was the last of the Big Three to venture into feature-length films. Chaplin made *The Kid* in 1921, and Harold Lloyd's first designated feature *Grandma's Boy* was released in 1922. *Three Ages* was the last film Buster made with former Keystone Kops actor and director Eddie Cline until 1940 when Cline generously called on a struggling Buster to appear in a supporting role in *The Villain Still Pursued Her*. However, Cline would work with Buster again on *The Buster Keaton Show* in 1950. He also went on to direct a handful of W.C. Fields films, including *The Bank Dick* and *Never Give a Sucker an Even Break*.

The American Film Institute catalogues the release date as August 1923. Some prints do not credit Eddie Cline as director.

Our Hospitality

Directed by: Buster Keaton, Jack Blystone
Produced by: Joseph M. Schenck
Presented by: Joseph M. Schenck
Story by: Jean Havez, Clyde Bruckman, Joseph Mitchell, Buster Keaton (uncredited)
Released: 19 November 1923
Premiere: 3 October 1923, San Francisco
Length: 74 minutes (7 reels, 6,220 feet)

Cast:
Buster Keaton – Willie McKay, 21 years old
Joe Roberts – Joseph Canfield
Ralph Bushman – Clayton Canfield, his 1st son
Craig Ward – Lee Canfield, his 2nd son
Monte Collins – Rev. Benjamin Dorsey, the parson
Joe Keaton – Lem Doolittle, the engineer
Kitty Bradbury – Mary, the aunt
Natalie Talmadge – Virginia Canfield, the girl
Buster Keaton Jr. – Willie McKay, 1 year old
Jim Blackwell – Canfield servant (uncredited)
Leonard Clapham – James Canfield (uncredited)

(Some character names are taken from the review in *Motion Picture News* of 24 November 1923)

Erwin and Jane Connelly – Quarrelling couple (uncredited)
Edward Coxen – John McKay (uncredited)
Jack Duffy – Sam Gardner, the conductor (uncredited)
Jean Dumas – Mrs. McKay (uncredited)
George Marion – Traffic policeman (uncredited)

Photography: Gordon Jennings, Elgin Lessley
Art director: Fred Gabourie
Lighting: Denver Harmon
Costumes: Walter Israel
Production company: Buster Keaton Productions
Distributed by: Metro Pictures

A wild and stormy night in 1810 – the feud between the McKays and the Canfields culminates in John McKay and James Canfield shooting each other dead. McKay's wife decides to bring up their son Willie with her sister in the relative safety of New York City.

Twenty years later, Willie inherits the McKay estate. Travelling to his birthplace, he falls for a girl on the train, who naturally enough, though unbeknownst to him, is a Canfield. Having discovered his estate is a derelict house, he again chances upon the girl, who, unaware he is a McKay, invites him to supper at the Canfield mansion. When the truth is revealed, her brothers are all for shooting him on sight, but their father overrules, pointing out, quite reasonably, that to do so would go against "our hospitality".

The story is based on the real life feud between the Hatfield and McCoy clans in West Virginia/Kentucky in the late nineteenth century.

Shot in Truckee, the location for *The Frozen North*, in August and September 1923, it features three generations of Keaton boys, and is Buster's last film with Natalie. Their son plays the part of Buster's own character as a baby. On his birth Buster was delighted to hand down a family tradition and announce that, and for the sixth time, the first-born was named Joseph Keaton. Natalie preferred to call him Jimmy, and Buster was deeply hurt when she insisted this be his given name.

In the climactic scene where Buster is washed downstream, the wire securing him snapped and he was swept along uncontrollably toward life-threatening whitewater rapids. Fortunately he managed to hang onto waterside foliage until help arrived. His main concern was that the camera had kept rolling and captured the scene – which it had.

This scene in the movie ends with Buster tied to a rope and swinging pendulum-style across a waterfall to grab Natalie as she is swept over. This was done on the studio lot – actually what were the Robert Brunton Studios and is now the Paramount lot – where a waterfall was constructed with miniature trees in the background to give perspective. Although Buster performed the stunt himself, Natalie is substituted by a dummy. Stuntman Harvey Perry had doubled for Natalie earlier in the river sequence.

The bicycle used in the film is such an accurate copy of the original so-called Gentleman's Hobby-Horse cycle from the 1820s that the Smithsonian Institution wrote to Buster in December 1923 asking if he would donate it to them. He replied that he was "keenly elated" to do so.

The Gentleman's Hobby-Horse

Early reports of filming gave the title as *Heading South*. The film was premiered in the UK in October 1923 and in San Francisco on 8 November, in both cases as a six-reel film called *Hospitality*. The copyright date for *Our Hospitality* is 20 November 1923.

Leonard Clapham was soon to change his name to Tom London, and notch up over 600 appearances in films between 1915 and 1961. He is also alleged to have appeared in the landmark 1903 short film *The Great Train Robbery*.

Costume designer Walter Israel is sometimes billed as Walter Isreal.

This was Joe Roberts' eighteenth and last film with Buster. He suffered a stroke during filming and was hospitalised in Reno, Nevada. A double was used for a number of scenes in the meantime. He insisted on returning to the film when he was able, but a month after shooting his final scene he suffered a further stroke and died.

Sherlock Jr.

Directed by: Buster Keaton, Roscoe "Fatty" Arbuckle (uncredited, some scenes), Donald Crisp (uncredited)
Produced by: Joseph M. Schenck, Buster Keaton (uncredited)
Presented by: Joseph M. Schenck
Written by: Jean Havez, Joseph Mitchell, Clyde Bruckman, Buster Keaton (uncredited)
Released: 21 April 1924
Length: 44 minutes (5 reels, 4,065 feet)

Cast:
Buster Keaton – Projectionist / Sherlock, Jr.
Kathryn McGuire – The girl
Joe Keaton – The girl's father / Man on film screen
Erwin Connelly – The hired man / The butler
Ward Crane – The local sheik / The villain
Jane Connelly – The mother (uncredited)
George Davis – Conspirator (uncredited)
Doris Deane – Girl who loses dollar outside cinema (uncredited)
Chrystine Francis – Candy store girl (uncredited)
Horace Morgan – Conspirator (uncredited)
Steve Murphy – Conspirator (uncredited)
John Patrick – Conspirator (uncredited)
Ford West – Theatre manager / Gillette (uncredited)
Betsy Ann Hisle – Little girl (uncredited) (unconfirmed)

Photography by: Elgin Lessley, Byron Houck
Edited by: Buster Keaton (uncredited)   Art director: Fred Gabourie
Electrician: Denver Harmon   Costumes: Clare West
Production company: Buster Keaton Productions
Distributed by: Metro Pictures

Projectionist and amateur sleuth Buster spends his last dollar buying chocolates for his girl. Not to be outdone, Buster's rival for the girl's affections steals her father's pocket watch and pawns it to buy her a box of chocolates at thrice the price. When the theft is discovered, the rival ensures that the blame falls on Buster, who sets out to clear his name. On returning to his day job, he dreams he is the renowned detective Sherlock Jr., called in to trace a set of stolen pearls. After much derring-do he cracks the case, and wakes to find his girl has discovered the truth of the missing pocket watch.

That Roscoe Arbuckle had a hand in directing *Sherlock Jr.* is pretty much a given, although the extent of his involvement is debatable. Buster told Kevin Brownlow in 1964 that he asked Roscoe to direct the film as he was still out of work following the scandal of 1921. However, according to Buster, Roscoe was still emotionally shattered by his near-conviction for murder, was irritable and difficult to work with. Buster remembered that he eased him out of the director's chair after three days and restarted the film from scratch. On the other hand, Doris Deane, the girl who loses the dollar outside the theatre, and who would become Roscoe Arbuckle's second wife the following year, claimed that Roscoe directed the whole picture. The truth surely lies somewhere between, and it's likely that scenes substantially directed by Roscoe remain in the film. What casts a little doubt on Buster's recollection is that he claimed Roscoe left the picture having received an offer to work on the Marion Davies picture *The Red Mill*, but work on *The Red Mill* did not start until 1926.

For some time while in production, the film was to be called *The Misfit*.

The scheduled release date of 10 March was inevitably missed when filming went on until the beginning of that month. At a preview in April the film ran to around 4,500 feet.

Ward Crane was a good friend of Buster's, and was best man at his wedding.

As an echo of the structure of *Three Ages*, which consisted of three 20-minute stories that were interwoven and could have been split to form three separate two-reelers, *Sherlock Jr.* has a symmetrical form of "inner" and "outer" stories, both of about 22 minutes.

Apart from "the world's greatest detective" himself, the only named character is Sherlock Jr.'s sidekick, Gillette. The intertitle "A Gem who was Ever-Ready in a bad scrape" is a reference to the Gillette Ever Ready safety razor that was popular at the time. It is probably also a nod to the actor William Gillette, renowned for playing Sherlock Holmes on stage. His only film, the lead in *Sherlock Holmes* (1916), was rediscovered in 2016 having been thought lost.

Buster switches roles for the stunt at the beginning of the driverless motor bike sequence. Buster has leapt onto the handlebars of a motorcycle ridden by his trusty servant Gillette. Almost immediately, the cycle hits a bump and Gillette falls off, but Buster, facing forwards, carries on, assuming that his sidekick is still in control of the bike. For the fall, the two changed places and it is Buster who takes the fall.

Sherlock Jr. is also notable for a stunt that truly made its mark on Buster. He is running along the roof of a moving locomotive, and, to avoid falling off the back, grabs hold of the spout of a water tank that is used to refill the steam engine boilers. In pulling the spout down Buster had underestimated the force of the torrent of water that was released, which knocked him to the ground, hitting his head against the rails. The scene continues with him getting to his feet and running off into the distance. Shooting was suspended for a couple of days as Buster was suffering from bad headaches, but these eventually subsided and filming could continue. Twelve years later, while undergoing a full medical examination, the doctor examining his X-rays asked him when it was that he broke his neck. "Never," Buster replied. The doctor pointed out on the X-ray where an old break had healed over. Buster reasoned that it must have been that day under the waterspout that without realising it, he had broken his neck.

The brief scene with a couple of lions tested Buster's braveness to the limit. Having been told not make any sudden moves that might startle the lions, Buster was understandably nervous during the shooting of the scene to the extent he forgot where the camouflaged exit from the cage was located. Having completed the scene there would usually be a second take to create a separate negative for making a foreign language version. Buster was in no mood to re-enter the lions' den and decided that the European market would be spared the scene. In the event, a copy of the domestic negative was made.

Some of the special camera effects are discussed in the section on camera techniques "Twenty-five Busters and Other Marvels" on p. 55. The film boasts a myriad of other less obvious effects. One such is where Buster, seated on the handlebars of a motorcycle unaware that no one is steering the machine, races towards a rail crossing and misses an oncoming locomotive by inches. This sequence was shot with the film being cranked backwards – the motor bike was being pulled backwards (out of sight of the camera of course) towards the crossing and the locomotive steaming away in reverse – allowing the "miss" to be more accurately judged.

Cameraman Byron Houck was one of a number of baseball professionals who Buster recruited for his films. He had been a pitcher for the Philadelphia Athletics, and was playing for the Vernon Tigers when Roscoe Arbuckle bought the team in 1919 – even though Roscoe himself had no real affinity for the game. He installed his business manager Lou Anger as the team's manager. Houck was married to Kittye Issacs, whose sister, vaudeville entertainer Sophye Barnard, was married to … Lou Anger. It was when Kittye died in 1923 and Houck's baseball career wound down that he joined Buster's film crew.

Buster previewed the film three times, cutting and reshooting after reading audience comments each time. *Variety* reported that around 60,000 feet of film were shot, trimmed to 5,000 feet, and finally to just over 4,000 feet. Sixteen millimetre Audio-Brandon prints were said to exist that included a scene towards the end where Buster went back for Gilette, apparently cut for the official release.

The American Film Institute lists the film's release date as 11 May.

The Navigator

Directed by: Donald Crisp, Buster Keaton
Produced by: Buster Keaton
Presented by: Joseph M. Schenck
Story by: Clyde Bruckman, Joseph Mitchell, Jean Havez, Buster Keaton
  (uncredited)
Released: 13 October 1924
Premiere: 12 October 1924, New York
Length: 59 minutes (6 reels, 5,600 feet)

Cast:
Buster Keaton – Rollo Treadway
Kathryn McGuire – Betsy O'Brien
Frederick Vroom – John O'Brien
Clarence Burton – Spy (uncredited)
H.M. Clugston – Spy (uncredited)
Jean Havez – Submarine cook (uncredited)
Noble Johnson – Cannibal chief (uncredited)
John Sinclair – Submarine navigator (uncredited)

Photography by: Elgin Lessley, Byron Houck
Technical director: Fred Gabourie
Electrician: Denver Harmon
Production company: Buster Keaton Productions
Distributed by: Metro-Goldwyn Distributing

> Wealthy Rollo Treadway – "living proof that every family tree must have its sap" – decides on a whim to propose to his neighbour, the equally wealthy Betsy O'Brien. Undeterred by her refusal, he sets off on his equally impulsively planned honeymoon trip anyway. By a rotten stroke of luck, he drives past the dock where the honeymoon liner is moored and instead boards the *Navigator*, which Betsy's father had just sold to a foreign power at war. A further rotten stroke of luck finds Betsy on board just as the foreign power's enemies cut the ship adrift. The *Navigator*'s sole passengers eventually find each other as the ship drifts out into the Pacific and towards a tropical island inhabited by cannibals.

The *Navigator* was in fact the 5,000-ton 500-foot SS *Buford* which belonged to the Alaskan Siberian Navigation Company and which was docked at San Francisco prior to being scrapped. Fred Gabourie had been asked by director Frank Lloyd to track down a four-masted schooner for his production of *The Sea Hawk*. In the process he came across the *Buford*, and informed Buster, resulting in Buster Keaton Productions leasing it for $25,000.

Buster was less than happy with director Donald Crisp, who seemed more interested in becoming a gagman than a straight director, and allowed the actors in the prologue to overact shamelessly. Having told Crisp that he could leave because the picture was finished, Buster then re-shot the sequence. It was reported at the time that there was also a disagreement between Buster and Crisp over the underwater scenes. Crisp was against any underwater footage being filmed, and so, according to *Variety*, as with the prologue, after Buster had told Crisp that filming was complete and he had left the lot, Buster shot the whole underwater sequence himself.

Crisp left his mark on the film, however – his is the angry face on the portrait that swings into view outside Rollo's porthole. He went on to become a character actor of note, appearing in a raft of films including *National Velvet*, *Wuthering Heights* and *How Green Was My Valley*, for which he won an Oscar for Best Supporting Actor.

The underwater scenes were the most expensive sequence to be shot. This was intended to be filmed in a swimming pool in Riverside, but when this failed to work out, the production hiked 500 miles north to the crystal clear – but ice-cold – waters of Lake Tahoe.

Variety reported in August 1924 that several thousand feet of film for underwater scenes had been shot, but this was cut to about 1,000 feet for the first preview. As the scenes were still felt to drag this was cut further so that "at present only about 500 feet remain, with the possibility that before the release of the picture this will be reduced."

Commercially, the film was Buster's most successful, grossing up to ten times its original budget, depending on whose figures you believe. It made just under $28,000 in two days at one cinema – the famous Capitol Theatre at 1645 Broadway in New York – a record at the time.

Although Metro-Goldwyn-Mayer had been formed when the film was released, it was billed as a Metro-Goldwyn Attraction. The American Film Institute database credits the producer as Joseph M. Schenck and the production company as Metro-Goldwyn Pictures.

Seven Chances

Directed by: Buster Keaton
Produced by: Buster Keaton, Joseph M. Schenck
Presented by: Joseph M. Schenck
Screen version by: Clyde Bruckman, Jean Havez, Joseph Mitchell, Buster Keaton
  (uncredited)
Adapted from David Belasco's famous comedy by Roi Cooper Megrue
Released: 16 March 1925
Length: 56 minutes (6 reels, 5,113 feet)

Cast:
Buster Keaton – James Shannon
T. Roy Barnes – Billy Meekin, his partner
Snitz Edwards – His lawyer
Ruth Dwyer – Mary Jones, his girl
Frankie Raymond – Mrs. Jones, her mother
Erwin Connelly – The clergyman
Jules Cowles – The hired man
Eugenia Gilbert – 1st chance: girl in big hat (uncredited)
Doris Deane – 2nd chance: girl proposed to on golf course (uncredited)
Judy King – 3rd chance: shredder of 'Will You Marry Me' note (uncredited)
Hazel Deane – 4th chance: the refuser (uncredited)
Bartine Burkett – 5th chance: country club girl (uncredited)
Connie Evans – 6th chance: country club girl (uncredited)
Pauline Toller – 7th chance: country club girl (uncredited)
Jean Arthur – Miss Smith, switchboard operator (uncredited)
Lori Bara – Mother of underage girl (uncredited)
Rosalind Byrne – Hat-check girl (uncredited)
Louise Carver – Prospective bride who operates crane (uncredited)
Rosa Gore – Prospective bride at church (uncredited)
Edna Hammon (uncredited)
Marion Harlan – Girl proposed to while driving (uncredited)

Jean Havez – Man getting off elevator (uncredited)
Rosalind Mooney – Prospective bride at church (uncredited)
Barbara Pierce – Prospective bride at church (uncredited)
Kate Price – Prospective bride at church (uncredited)
Billy Rinaldi – Boy (uncredited)
Julian Rivero – Barber (uncredited)
S.D. Wilcox – Policeman (uncredited)

Photography by: Elgin Lessley, Byron Houck
Art director: Fred Gabourie
Electrician: Denver Harmon
Production company: Buster Keaton Productions
Distributed by: Metro-Goldwyn Pictures

Buster's biographer Ed McPherson puts it impeccably: "the premise of *Seven Chances* is best swallowed whole". Financial broker Jimmy Shannon's firm is on the brink of ruin. In the nick of time Jimmy finds out that his grandfather has left him $7 million – if he is married by 7pm on his 27th birthday. A glance at the desk calendar confirms to Jimmy that his 27th birthday is indeed today. Having been rejected by seven women in his club's dining room, Jimmy resorts to placing an advertisement in a local paper, inviting potential brides to meet at Broad St. Church at 5pm. Hordes of women of every description turn up, including at least one who is clearly a man. On hearing the clergyman dismiss the whole thing as a practical joke, the thwarted brides turn on Jimmy en masse.

Seven Chances marked the fifth and final collaboration between the dream team of writers Clyde Bruckman, Jean Havez and Joseph Mitchell. Only Bruckman would work with Buster again, including on *The Buster Keaton Show* in the 1950s. Havez died of a heart attack before *Seven Chances* was released. His widow Ebba married Eddie Sedgwick in 1933.

The prologue is filmed in two-strip Technicolor.

Joe Schenck bought the rights to David Belasco's play "Seven Chances" for $25,000 without consulting Buster, who had seen the play on Broadway in 1916 and considered it a non-credible farce. As a result, he was always dismissive of the film, but revised his opinion very late in life when Raymond Rohauer bought up the rights and, having not been seen in over 35 years, it was screened to great success at the 1965 New York Film Festival.

Part of the deal struck by Joe Schenck was that John McDermott would direct the film. McDermott left the film after just two weeks, but apparently on good terms. The reason was supposedly for overspending, but the problem was as much artistic differences. He had wanted to film a farce, but Buster insisted on gags – "You are the star and producer, and your version will be the one finally used," he told Buster.

Filming took place between September and November in various locations around Hollywood, and in Burbank and Newhall, north of Los Angeles. The country club set was later used as the department store in *Go West*.

The female impersonator gag involves Julian Eltinge, who would certainly have been well known to audiences at the time. He made his name in vaudeville before moving into films, notably in *The Isle of Love* with Rudolph Valentino and Virginia Rappe.

Constance Talmadge is often credited as appearing as a passenger in a car, but she almost certainly is not in the film.

The cascading rock scene was shot after a preview audience began to laugh when Buster accidentally dislodged a rock when running downhill. He realised the audience were expecting the rock to have a knock-on effect and start an avalanche, whereas the scene quickly faded. He set up a re-shoot on a steeper hill in the High Sierras with hundreds of papier-mâché rocks of all sizes to create what became the most memorable scene in the film.

However, Buster's personal favourite shot, and one of the most elegant effects he and Elgin Lessley ever achieved, was of the drive from the country house to Mary's house and back. He climbs into the car and sits behind the wheel, but doesn't move. Instead the background fades from one location to the next, at which point he climbs out of the car. A lovely image, but of course not a straightforward one to film – Buster later explained to Kevin Brownlow that surveyors' instruments were needed to ensure the car was perfectly positioned for each transition, even matching the slight incline of the roads. As ever, huge effort and great ingenuity for just a few seconds of film.

Go West

Directed by: Buster Keaton
Produced by: Joseph M. Schenck
Presented by: Joseph M. Schenck
Written by: Buster Keaton, Lex Neal
Scenario: Raymond Cannon
Released: 1 November 1925
Length: 69 minutes (7 reels, 6,256/6,295 feet)

Cast:
Buster Keaton – Friendless
Howard Truesdale – Owner of the Diamond Bar ranch
Kathleen Myers – His daughter
Ray Thompson – The foreman
Brown Eyes – Herself
Roscoe Arbuckle – Woman in department store (uncredited)
Erwin Connelly – Stockyard owner
Joe Keaton – Man in barber shop (uncredited)
Gus Leonard – General store owner (uncredited)
Babe London – Woman in department store (uncredited)

Photography: Elgin Lessley, Bert Haines
Art direction: Fred Gabourie
Electrical effects: Denver Harmon
Production company: Buster Keaton Productions
Distributed by: Metro-Goldwyn[-Mayer] Pictures

A drifter, whom we'll call Friendless, unable to find work in the city, heeds the advice of *Tribune* editor Horace Greeley and Goes West. Despite a complete lack of experience, he gets a job at a cattle ranch. He earns a friend for life in the form of a cow, whom we'll call Brown Eyes, by removing a rock that had been jammed in her hoof. On hearing that the ranch owner is about to send the entire herd to the stockyard, Friendless goes to extreme and unlikely lengths to protect his loyal friend.

Co-writer Lex Neal, a friend of Buster from The Three Keatons days, also acted as assistant director – indeed when filming began, Neal was reported as being the director.

The names of the leads seem to have been taken from the characters of The Friendless One and Brown Eyes in D.W. Griffith's 1916 epic *Intolerance*. A

Buster and
Brown Eyes

subtle point that was evidently lost on *Variety*, who credited Buster's character as "The Drifter".

Buster trained Brown Eyes to follow him by initially leading her around with a halter rope. Then over a period of ten days the rope was substituted for a smaller rope, then a cord, and finally a black cotton thread, which was all but invisible on screen.

Roscoe Arbuckle makes a heavily disguised but conspicuously bulky cameo appearance as one of two large women taking refuge from the swarming cattle by heading for the lift of the department store. He was still banned from appearing on screen at the time, but Buster was obviously feeling reckless and in the mood to cock a snook at the Hays Office. Roscoe's characteristic arm-waving reaction to the approaching herd is unmistakable.

A rethink of the final scene was necessary when it became apparent that the steers were refusing to chase Buster in his red devil costume. For whatever reason, as soon as he started to move, they stopped still. Even clever editing could not create the impression of the hoped-for climactic stampede, which probably contributed to Buster's ultimate disappointment in the film as a whole.

Filming took place in June, north of Kingman and in nearby Hackberry, Arizona, with city shots in Hollywood and downtown Los Angeles. The film premiered in New York on 25 October 1925.

Battling Butler

Directed by: Buster Keaton
Produced by: Joseph M. Schenck
Presented by: Joseph M. Schenck
Adapted from the stage success of the
    same name by Paul Gerard Smith, Al
    Boasberg, Charles H. Smith, Lex Neal

From the play "Battling Buttler" by
    Stanley Brightman, Austin Melford
New York premiere: 22 August 1926
Released: September 1926
Length: 71 minutes (7 reels,
    6,970 feet)

Cast:
Buster Keaton – Alfred Butler
Snitz Edwards – His valet
Sally O'Neil – The mountain girl
Walter James – Her father
Budd Fine – Her brother
Francis McDonald – Alfred Battling Butler
Mary O'Brien – His wife
Tom Wilson – His trainer
Eddie Borden – His manager
Al Boasberg – Bandleader at wedding (uncredited)
Lillian Lawrence – Aunt at wedding (uncredited)

Photography by: Dev Jennings [as J.D. Jennings], Bert Haines
Technical director: Fred Gabourie
Electrical effects: Ed Levy
Production company: Buster Keaton Productions
Distributed by: Metro-Goldwyn-Mayer Distributing Corp.

Alfred Butler, as wealthy as he is indolent, is sent into the mountains by his father in order that he be made a man of. Fortunately his valet is on hand to take the edge off mountain life by cooking his breakfast, running his bath, laying out his clothes, and seeing to other such essential activities. Alfred falls for a mountain girl, but her father and brother scorn his foppishness. As luck would have it, the valet reads in the morning paper of a prizefighter who shares a name with our hero. He wins the mocking pair round by pointing out that his employer is none other than – Alfred "Battling" Butler.

Which just leaves the small matter of "Battling" Butler's upcoming fight against the Alabama Murderer.

Battling Butler was linked with Buster as early as 1924 – *Film Daily* of 17 March revealed that Joe Schenck was being tipped by many to acquire the screen rights of the play for Buster. The rights for the film were eventually acquired early in 1925, but the deal was then temporarily cancelled due to the stipulation that the film could be shown everywhere apart from England. Such was the certainty that Buster would be in the film that in June 1925 the same *Film Daily* rather tied itself in knots by describing Lex Neal as being engaged in "co-direction with Buster Keaton on *Brown Eyes*, an adaptation of *Mr. Battling Butler*".

Battling Butler was shot between January and March – Buster was injured when filming a boxing scene in February. It was mostly filmed in a town called Kernville, which no longer exists as it was submerged when the Lake Isabella dam

was built in 1948. Buster's mansion was shot at the Talmadge apartment building on Wilshire Boulevard, Los Angeles. The building is believed to have been built by Joe Schenck for his wife Norma Talmadge.

Buster was evidently fond of the duck-shooting scene and reworked it as a short filmed insert for his touring production *Merton of the Movies* in 1957.

The film premiered in New York on 22 August 1926. It was the last of Buster's films to be distributed by MGM until *The Cameraman*.

Al Boasberg was a vaudeville writer who was signed on by Joseph Schenck as a gag man and scenario writer for Buster for a six-week probationary period with an option for a year. After writing for *Battling Butler* and *The General*, he left Buster Keaton Productions – although on such good terms he placed an ad in *Variety* thanking Buster "for your kindness and acceptance of my comedy suggestions". The problem, as Buster explained in *My Wonderful World of Slapstick*, was that Boasberg was a master of verbal firecracker wit, but was hopeless at sight gags. (A delicious example between Buster and Mary O'Brien, who plays his rival's wife, after she had had trouble with both her husband and her shoe: "How's your heel?" "Oh, he's all right.") Boasberg would work with Buster again, however, unofficially on *The Cameraman* and officially on *Doughboys* and *Free and Easy*.

Cameraman Dev Jennings joined Buster for the first of four films. Jennings was partially blind in his right eye, possibly as the result of playing with gunpowder when aged seven. He was the elder brother of Gordon Jennings, the cameraman on *Our Hospitality*.

Having just finished filming *El Moderno Barba Azul* in Mexico in 1946, Buster began work on a remake of *Battling Butler* with Clyde Bruckman, again to be shot in Mexico. Although he completed the script in 1947, nothing came of it.

A variety of release dates are on offer – the American Film Institute gives August 1926, others plump specifically for 22 August. Most give 4 or 19 September, including Eleanor Keaton's memoir, which gives 19 September.

The General

Directed by: Buster Keaton, Clyde Bruckman
Produced by: Joseph M. Schenck
Presented by: Joseph M. Schenck
Written by: Buster Keaton, Clyde Bruckman
Adapted by: Al Boasberg, Charles Smith
Based on *The Great Locomotive Chase* by William Pittenger (originally published in 1863 as *Daring and Suffering, a History of the Great Railroad Adventurers*)
Released: 5 February 1927
Premiere: 22 December 1926, Los Angeles; 31 December 1926, Tokyo; 17 January 1927, London; 5 (or 6) February 1927, New York
Length: 75 minutes (8 reels, 7,500 feet)

Cast:
Buster Keaton – Johnnie Gray
Marion Mack – Annabelle Lee
Glen Cavender – Captain Anderson
Jim Farley – General Thatcher
Frederick Vroom – A Southern General
Charles Smith – Annabelle's father
Frank Barnes – Annabelle's brother
Joe Keaton – Union General
Mike Donlin – Union Major
Tom Nawn – Union Lieutenant Colonel
Henry Baird – Soldier (uncredited)
Joe Bricher – Soldier (uncredited)
Jimmy Bryant – Raider (uncredited)
Sergeant Bukowski – Officer (uncredited)
C.C. Cruson – Officer (uncredited)
Jack Dempster – Raider (uncredited)
Keith Fennell – Soldier (uncredited)
Budd Fine – Raider (uncredited)
Eddie Foster – Union railroad fireman (uncredited)
Ronald Gilstrap – Union soldier (uncredited)
Frank Hagney – Confederate recruiter (uncredited)
Ray Hanford – Raider (uncredited)
Jack Hanlon – Boy who follows Johnny (uncredited)
Al Hanson – Raider (or Al Handon, uncredited)
Anthony Harvey – Raider (uncredited)
Edward Hearn – Union officer (uncredited)
Dev Jennings – Union General giving command to cross bridge (uncredited)
Hilliard Karr – Soldier (uncredited)
Louis Lewyn – Soldier (uncredited)
Jackie Lowe – Boy who follows Johnny (uncredited)

Billy Lynn – Soldier (uncredited)
Ross McCutcheon – Raider (uncredited)
Tom Moran – Raider (uncredited)
Charles Phillips – Raider (uncredited)
Red Rial – Raider (uncredited)
Al St. John – Officer on horseback (uncredited)
Harold Terry – Union soldier (uncredited)
Ray Thomas – Raider (uncredited)
Red Thompson – Raider (uncredited)
James Walsh – Soldier (uncredited)
Kenneth Hawley Ward – Soldier (uncredited)
John Wilson – Union soldier (uncredited)
Gene Woodward (or Jean Woodward, uncredited)
Boris Karloff – Union General (uncredited) (unconfirmed)

Photographed by: Dev Jennings, Bert Haines
Edited by: Buster Keaton, Sherman Kell
Technical director: Fred Gabourie
Lighting effects: Denver Harmon
Production company: Buster Keaton Productions
Distributed by: United Artists

> Johnnie Gray has two loves, being, in no particular order, his girl Annabelle Lee and his locomotive *The General*. War breaks out and Johnnie tries to enlist, but the recruiting officer decides he is more use as a civilian train engineer than as a soldier. Unfortunately he fails to tell Johnnie this, and so Annabelle and her family assume he is a coward and want nothing more to do with him. One year later, Union spies steal *The General* intending to head north, destroying the South's communication and supply lines en route. That Annabelle happens to be aboard *The General* gives Johnnie added incentive to recapture his locomotive. This he does with aplomb, outwitting his pursuers with equal parts luck and ingenuity.

The film is based on the real life hijacking of the locomotive *The General* in 1862, and its use to sabotage Confederate communication links in the American Civil War, as recounted by William Pittenger, one of the raiders, in a book published the following year. Buster switched the perspective of the book, which was written from the point of view of the Northern raiders, and told the story of the Confederate engineer of the hijacked train. He added two key aspects to the story – the second locomotive chase, and the love interest. Buster initially rejected as "without foundation" a law suit brought by Mrs. Winnie C. Pittenger in July 1927 claiming he lifted the plot from her late husband's book.

The fade-out of the first sequence is one of the film's most memorable scenes. It sees a dejected Buster sitting on the driving bar of *The General*, realising only as he disappears into a roundhouse that the engine is moving and his distracted body has been moving in a series of graceful arcs. This was also one of the riskiest scenes in the film. The train driver told him: "A fraction too much steam with these old-fashioned engines and the wheel spins. And if it spins it will kill you right then and there."

Location filming took place in Cottage Grove, Oregon, between June and August 1926. Battle scenes that were shot towards the end of filming may have triggered extensive forest fires, although the area was experiencing a 60-day drought, with temperatures of up to 40 degrees, and so there may have been any number of unrelated forest fires. In any event, the lingering smoke meant some outstanding scenes could not be filmed on schedule. Buster and members of his crew returned to Cottage Grove in early September once the smoke had cleared to complete filming.

The scene showing the *Texas*, the locomotive pursuing *The General* at the climax of the film, crossing a burning trestle bridge and plunging 35 feet into the river is reckoned to be the most expensive single shot in silent movie history, costing some $42,000 (around $620,000 today). It was filmed at Culp Creek in Oregon on 23 July 1926, where Fred Gabourie and his crew had built a full-size trestle bridge over the Row River. The original intention had been to use an existing bridge, but as no suitable location could be found the decision was made three weeks before the scene was shot that a bridge would be built specifically for the purpose. The collapse was clearly meticulously planned as it is timed to perfection, and there is added poignancy in the engine's whistle

blowing out a clear jet of steam from amid the crumpled wreckage of the loco-motive. The smashed locomotive remained a tourist attraction until it was sal-vaged for scrap metal during the Second World War.

Elgin Lessley is sometimes said to be the General who orders the *Texas* to cross the bridge, but Dev Jennings does the honours here.

Glen Cavender, who plays Union Captain Anderson, was a much-decorated war hero. For his activities in the Philippines, the China Boxer expedition and Puerto Rico, he held the Congressional Medal, the Medal for Valor and the Medal for Conspicuous Bravery, as well as the Chevalier of the Legion d'Honneur for saving the life of a French Marshall in Peking. He was a major in the First World War, and received further decorations, including the French Croix de Guerre.

Snitz Edwards appeared in the scene where Johnny Gray is exposed as a spy, but he was cut from the film. It was also Marion Mack's last feature film – she later explained that her husband didn't like her being away from home.

Although officially released on 5 February, US screenings outside Los Angeles began from 15 January.

The film was not well received, critically or by the public, probably because a comedy was anticipated, and the film is as dramatic as it is comedic. The headline for the *Los Angeles Times* review of 12 March 1927 sums up the feel-ing: "Comedy Is Lost In War Incidents". Opinions have changed of course and in 2007 it was voted number 18 on the American Film Institute's list of best American films of all time.

In January 1927 it was announced that Buster's follow-up to *The General* would be *The Poor Fish* with Edith Roberts. According to *Variety*, Sam Taylor as direc-tor and Tim Whelan and Carl Harbaugh as writers were on loan to Buster from Mary Pickford at United Artists to work on the film. Within two weeks the same publication announced Buster's new project was "a college story as yet untitled".

College

Directed by: James W. Horne, Buster Keaton (uncredited)
Produced by: Joseph M. Schenck
Presented by: Joseph M. Schenck
Story by: Carl Harbaugh, Bryan Foy
Titles by: Ralph Spence (uncredited)
Supervised by: Harry Brand
Released: 10 September 1927
Length: 65 minutes (6 reels, 5,916 feet)

Cast:
Buster Keaton – Ronald, a son
Anne Cornwall – The girl
Flora Bramley – Her friend
Harold Goodwin – A rival
Snitz Edwards – The Dean
Carl Harbaugh – Crew coach
Sam Crawford – Baseball coach
Florence Turner – A mother
Lee Barnes – Athlete (uncredited)
Robert Boling – Athlete (uncredited)
Charles Borah – Athlete (uncredited)
Leighton Dye – Athlete (uncredited)
Paul Goldsmith – Athlete (uncredited)
Kenneth Grumbles – Athlete (uncredited)
Charlie Hall – Coxswain (uncredited)
Bud Houser – Athlete (uncredited)
Morton Kaer – Athlete (uncredited)
Eric Mack – Athlete (uncredited)
James T. Mack – High school principal (uncredited)
Buddy Mason – Jeff's friend (uncredited)
Madame Sul-Te-Wan – Cook (uncredited)
USC Baseball Team – Themselves (uncredited)
Grant Withers – Jeff's friend (uncredited)
Shorty Worden – Athlete (uncredited)

Photographed by: Dev Jennings, Bert Haines
Film editor: Sherman Kell
Lighting effects by: Jack Lewis
Technical director: Fred Gabourie
Production company: Buster Keaton Productions
Distributed by: United Artists

In an effort to woo spunky Mary Haynes ("winner of every popularity contest in which the boys were allowed to vote"), bookish Ronald enrols at the sporting Clayton college. Delightfully inept as a soda jerk, and equally inept in an unfortunate scene as a blacked up "colored" waiter, it's no surprise that he fails to shine in every sporting discipline he tackles. Nevertheless, in a misguided attempt to help him win the girl, the sympathetic college Dean appoints him cox of the rowing crew. Although once again he's something of a disaster on the water, Ronald's latent athletic abilities surface triumphantly when he hears that Mary is in true peril.

Early publicity for the film gave the title as *Hercules the Weak*. Filming took place between February and July on the campus of the University of Southern California and the Los Angeles memorial Coliseum, with the boating scenes filmed at Balboa Park, Newport Beach.

Buster's incompetence as a soda jerk contrasts nicely with Roscoe's dexterity at the beginning of *His Wedding Night*.

One of the few stunts Buster didn't perform in his films was the final vault into the window of Mary's room. He felt it would take him too long to master the pole vaulting technique and was happy to leave it to professional Lee Barnes on this occasion.

Lee Barnes
doubles for Buster

In 1927 Joe Schenck effected a personnel change that Buster would later determine as the point at which the storm clouds began to gather over his career. His friend from the vaudeville days, Lou Anger, was taken off Buster Keaton Productions and replaced as studio manager by Harry Brand, who was previously Al St. John's press agent. It was a move that began the undermining of Buster's artistic freedom.

Buster clashed with his new studio manager during filming, as Brand would try to get on the right side of producer Schenck by cutting costs where possible. On watching the released film for the first time at a Sacramento movie theatre, Buster was angered to see the credit "Supervised by HARRY BRAND" had been inserted without his knowledge.

He also had little time for director James W. Horne, who was suggested by Brand, describing him to Kevin Brownlow as "absolutely useless" and claiming to have directed practically all of *College* himself. However, Horne did go on to direct several Laurel and Hardy features.

Buster had embarked on a tour of personal appearances at picture houses in November 1927 to promote *College*, staging an act that included a "Salome"-style burlesque dance. He cancelled the tour after two weeks as the four shows a day (five on Saturdays and Sundays) were taking too great a toll on his body.

The American Film Institute credits the production company as Joseph M. Schenck Productions.

Steamboat Bill, Jr.

Directed by: Chas F. Reisner, Buster Keaton (uncredited)
Produced by: Joseph M. Schenck
Presented by: Joseph M. Schenck
Story by: Carl Harbaugh, Buster Keaton (uncredited)
Released: 12 May 1928
Premiere: 5 April 1928, Santa Maria, California
Length: 71 minutes (7 reels, 6,400 feet)

Cast:
Buster Keaton – William Canfield Jr.
Tom McGuire – J.J. King
Ernest Torrence – William "Steamboat Bill" Canfield
Tom Lewis – Tom Carter, first and last mate
Marion Byron – Kitty King, King's daughter
Ford West – Barber (uncredited)
James T. Mack – Minister (uncredited)

Photographed by: Dev Jennings, Bert Haines
Edited by: Sherman Kell (uncredited)
Technical director: Fred Gabourie
Assistant (technical) director: Sandy Roth
Production company: Buster Keaton Productions
Distributed by: United Artists

William "Steamboat Bill" Canfield runs the second best of two Mississippi river boat services. His delight at the prospect of meeting his son for the first time since he was a baby is dampened when he finally meets Junior, compounded by the fact that the lad is enamoured of the daughter of his rival, JJ King. The efforts of both fathers to keep the young lovers apart are on the verge of succeeding, when King has Bill Sr. thrown in jail for assault. Junior is in the process of springing his father from jail when a cyclone hits town.

When developing the story, Buster planned the final catastrophe to be a flood. However, his nemesis Harry Brand protested to producer Joe Schenck that not only would it be too expensive, but that it would be in poor taste as there had been great loss of life in a Mississippi flood that year. Buster agreed to compromise on a cyclone, although rebuilding of the sets cost an extra $35,000 anyway. And, he was pleased to discover, hurricanes and cyclones cause significantly greater loss of life in America every year than floods.

Although set on the Mississippi, filming took place in August 1927 at the more convenient location of California's Sacramento River near the town of Sacramento itself. Filming was then completed in October at Buster's studio in Los Angeles. Some contemporary magazines give the release date as July 1928.

Perhaps the most iconic shot Buster ever filmed takes place during the storm. Battered by the winds, Buster pauses to take stock in front of a two-storey house. As he rubs his neck, the front of the house crashes down on top of him – but he happens to be standing in the space where the first floor window falls and so escapes being crushed. This potentially lethal shot was obviously carefully planned, but nevertheless, given the wind machines raging all around, the possibility for error could not be completely eliminated. Buster related how he

had a clearance of two inches on each shoulder, and the facade missed the top of his head by two inches and the bottom of his heels by two inches. Director Chuck Reisner reportedly couldn't bear to look, and it is said that he was off in the corner of the lot, praying alongside a Christian Scientist. A nice image, but possibly an exaggeration.

As the two-ton structure crashes around him, Buster doesn't even flinch. Buster later said that if he hadn't been at such a low ebb due to the state of his marriage and career, he would never have risked the stunt.

Louise Keaton acted as Marion Byron's water double for the scenes in the river, as the 16-year-old actress couldn't swim.

Production was temporarily held up in August when Buster broke his nose, predictably enough while playing baseball.

Chuck Reisner insisted on Buster smiling in the very last shot as he swims to the riverbank with a minister in tow. Buster strongly objected, and so alternate versions were shot. The smiling version tested so badly with audiences that it was binned and the deadpan version used.

Although often billed as Reisner, the director's real name was Charles F. Riesner. He got on well with Buster and the two remained friends for many years.

Tom Lewis died in October 1927, less than two months after filming completed.

Although Carl Harbaugh is credited as having written *Steamboat Bill, Jr.*, his actual contribution is less than clear. In 1964, Kevin Brownlow asked Buster about what Harbaugh brought to his films. He replied, "He didn't write nothing. He was one of the most useless men I ever had on the scenario department. He wasn't a good gag man; he wasn't a good title writer; he wasn't a good story constructionist." Asked why Harbaugh got sole writing credit: "Well, we had to put somebody's name up …".

THE MGM YEARS

The Cameraman

Directed by: Edward Sedgwick, Buster Keaton (uncredited)
Produced by: Edward Sedgwick, Buster Keaton, Lawrence Weingarten (uncredited)
Presented by: Metro-Goldwyn-Mayer
Story by: Clyde Bruckman, Lew Lipton, Byron Morgan (uncredited)
Continuity by: Richard Schayer, Al Boasberg (uncredited)
Titles by: Joe Farnham
Released: September 1928
Length: 76 minutes (as currently available) (8 reels, 6,995 feet)

Cast:
Buster Keaton – Buster
Marceline Day – Sally
Harold Goodwin – Stagg
Sidney Bracey – Editor
Harry Gribbon – Cop
Richard Alexander – The big sea lion (uncredited)
Edward Brophy – Man in bath-house (uncredited)
Ray Cooke – Office worker (uncredited)
Vernon Dent – Man in tight bathing suit (uncredited)
William Irving – Photographer (uncredited)
Harry Keaton – Swimmer in pool (uncredited)
Louise Keaton – Swimmer in pool (uncredited)
Bert Moorhouse – Randall (uncredited)
Jack Raymond – Swimming pool attendant (uncredited)

Photographed by: Elgin Lessley, Reggie Lanning
Film editor: Hugh Wynn, Basil Wrangell (uncredited)
Settings by: Fred Gabourie
Wardrobe by: David Cox
Production company: Metro-Goldwyn-Mayer
Distributed by: Metro-Goldwyn-Mayer

Enamoured by MGM News Reel stenographer Sally, Buster trades in his street photography equipment for a movie camera and a career as a newsreel cameraman. His early newsreel attempts show he has a lot to learn, but his feelings for Sally are reciprocated and they spend a happy, event filled Sunday together. Sally tips him off about an impending Tong war in Chinatown, but all he seems to have picked up from the day's events is a pet monkey – he has forgotten to load the camera. Happily the monkey saves the day, and contrives to cement his relationship with Sally.

Although his move to MGM was reported in a variety of contemporary sources as having already taken place in late November 1927 – *Variety* of 23 November and *Moving Picture World* of 3 December 1927, for example – a currently available facsimile of the brief of Buster's $3,000 a week, two-year contract with the studio is dated 26 January 1928. He was contracted to make two pictures a year – any more would earn him $50,000 each. Buster Keaton Productions would receive 25 per cent of all profits from his films, and Joe Keaton was retained at $100 a week.

The move to MGM seemed propitious – *The Cameraman* was hugely successful and grossed twice as much as *Steamboat Bill, Jr.* Director Edward Sedgwick, another former Keystone Kop, worked with Buster for his next seven MGM films, the two apparently bonding over a mutual love of baseball and dislike of producer Irving Thalberg. Like Buster, Eddie Sedgwick's background was vaudeville, having been one of The Five Sedgwicks.

MGM would not countenance Buster's improvisatory way of working, and insisted everything be scripted in detail. Buster relates that six months of careful scripting by up to 22 screenwriters was finally heaped upon him. The only two unscripted scenes in *The Cameraman* were the delightfully inventive scene in the empty baseball stadium, and his battle with the piggy bank. That being said, when attempts to film in New York were made impossible by marauding fans, Buster was allowed to improvise the scenes he shot there and adapt other scenes to make them filmable on the studio lot back in Los Angeles.

Shooting began in New York at the Yankee Stadium and on Fifth Avenue on 12 April 1928, continuing on the MGM lot from 1 May until 25 June, with three days of reshoots from 4 August. The waterside shots were filmed at Venice Beach and Newport Beach. In May 1928, the film was still being trailed as *Snapshots*, written by Byron Morgan. Lawrence Weingarten was reported as supervising the "Tim McCoy western unit".

The bather who Buster battles with in the changing cubicle, Edward Brophy, was unit manager on all of Buster's MGM features, with the possible exception of *Sidewalks of New York*. Buster encouraged him to appear in front of the screen – to the extent that when MGM first loaned him out to another studio, Buster told him, "Now you are a real actor at last. You've been sold down the river." Brophy directed the German version of *Parlor, Bedroom and Bath*.

Stock footage used in the film features American heroes Charles Lindbergh and Gertrude Ederle, the first woman to swim the English Channel.

The film was long thought to be lost, the master having been destroyed in a disastrous fire in one of the MGM vaults in 1965 in which one person died. However, a copy turned up in Paris in 1968, and a high quality positive master copy then surfaced in 1991. But even combining the two versions, there are two scenes missing, which Buster describes in *My Wonderful World of Slapstick*.

In one, Buster films a character at the Ambassador Hotel with a chest covered with gold braid under the mistaken impression that he is some kind of high-ranking navy officer when he turns out to be the hotel doorman. In the other Buster films the launch of a ship, but places his camera on the launch cradle and ends up gliding into the sea in the wake of the vessel.

The Ambassador Hotel sequence is mentioned in the review in *Variety* of 19 September 1929. And although elements of these scenes are unofficially available in the form of poor quality clips, no known copy exists in a form that would be acceptable for official release.

The Criterion Blu-ray release from 2020 also uses as source material sequences that were used in the 1964 MGM compilation *The Big Parade of Comedy*.

After 23 shorts and seven features, this was Elgin Lessley's last film with Buster. And after nearly as many collaborations with Fred Gabourie, it was also the last time Buster would work with his trusty technical director. Lessley officially retired after *The Cameraman*, occasionally doing some uncredited camera work, whereas Gabourie was promoted to MGM's head of construction.

Spite Marriage

Directed by: Edward Sedgwick, Buster Keaton (uncredited)
Produced by: Edward Sedgwick, Buster Keaton
Presented by: Metro-Goldwyn-Mayer
Story by: Lew Lipton
Adaptation by: Ernest S. Pagano
Continuity by: Richard Shayer
Titles by: Robert Hopkins

Released: 6 April 1929
Length: 74 minutes (9 reels, 7,047 feet with synchronised sound; also 6,500 feet silent)

Cast:
Buster Keaton – Elmer Gantry
Dorothy Sebastian – Trilby Drew
Edward Earle – Lionel Benmore
Leila Hyams – Ethyl Norcrosse
William Bechtel – Nussbaum
John Byron – Scarzi
Joe Bordeaux – Rumrunner (uncredited)
Ray Cooke – The bellboy (uncredited)
Mike Donlin – Man in ship's engine room (uncredited)
Pat Harmon – Tugboat captain (uncredited)
Sydney Jarvis – Man in audience next to Elmer (uncredited)
Theodore Lorch – Actor as "Union Officer" (uncredited)
Hank Mann – Stage manager (uncredited)
Charles Sullivan – Tough sailor (uncredited)
Monte Westmore – Actor applying make-up (uncredited)

Photographed by: Reggie Lanning
Film editor: Frank Sullivan
Art director: Cedric Gibbons
Wardrobe by: David Cox
Production company: Metro-Goldwyn-Mayer
Distributed by: Metro-Goldwyn-Mayer

Elmer is infatuated with stage actress Trilby Drew. A humble pants presser by day, by night he dons a tuxedo to watch her every performance. However, she is in love with her co-star Lionel Benmore, who in turn carries a brightly burning torch for Ethyl Norcrosse. Out of spite for Lionel's interest in Ethyl, Trilby asks Elmer to marry her, but immediately regrets it. Her manager extricates her from the marriage, and the fates thrust Elmer on a yacht with a gang of rum runners. But the dictates of screenplay logic, and the need for a satisfactory ending, conspire to throw the two back together again.

Contemporary audiences would have noted the similarity between the lead characters' names and those of Lionel and Ethel Barrymore. Of added interest for astute modern audience members would be that the female lead is called Drew (also the maiden name of Lionel and Ethel's mother).

Buster wasn't responsible for the stunt involving the car driving off the jetty – that was stuntman Bob Rose.

Monte Westmore, who was the make-up artist for the film, appears as the actor applying his own make-up, whom Buster attempts to copy.

Buster quickly hit it off with Dorothy Sebastian and the pair embarked upon a two-year affair. By all accounts it was a non-exclusive, good natured relationship that ended when she wanted to be a wife rather than a mistress. She later married William "Hopalong Cassidy" Boyd, although the marriage ended in 1936.

Buster takes on the character of Elmer for the first time, highlighting how MGM misinterpreted Buster and set him off in a direction playing not entirely to his strengths. The various Elmers he plays tend to be clumsy, incompetent and slow-witted. They are put-upon characters who pull through by chance and despite the odds. However, his success was not built on playing such witless types, but naïve characters, artless and innocent, who are supple, inventive and irrepressible, taking life as it comes and making the best of inauspicious circumstances.

Although Buster lobbied MGM for the film to have sound, it was released without dialogue, but with a synchronised soundtrack of music and special effects. A separate silent version, which was somewhat shorter, was also released.

In *My Wonderful World of Slapstick*, Buster refers to the film as *Spite Wife*.

This was Buster's last film with Joe Bordeaux – who also appeared in Buster's debut film. Joe's name seems to be written equally often with and without a final x. Most contemporary sources use the longer version, and so have we.

The AFI listed the production company as Joseph M. Schenck Productions.

Free and Easy

Directed by: Edward Sedgwick, Buster Keaton (uncredited)
Produced by: Edward Sedgwick, Buster Keaton
Presented by: Metro-Goldwyn-Mayer
Scenario by: Richard Shayer
Adaptation by: Paul Dickey
Dialogue by: Al Boasberg
Released: 22 March 1930
Length: 92 minutes (10 reels, 8,413 feet)

Cast:
Buster Keaton – Elmer J. Butts
Anita Page – Elvira Plunkett
Trixie Friganza – Ma Plunkett
Robert Montgomery – Larry Mitchell
Fred Niblo – Himself, Director Niblo
Edgar Dearing – Officer
Gwen Lee – Herself, actress in bedroom scene
John Miljan – Himself, actor in bedroom scene

Lionel Barrymore – Himself, director of bedroom scene
William Haines – Himself, guest at premiere
William Collier Sr. – Himself, Master of Ceremonies
Dorothy Sebastian – Herself, actress in cave scene
Karl Dane – Himself, actor in cave scene
David Burton – Himself, Director Burton
Jack Baxley – Train conductor (uncredited)
Edward Brophy – Benny, the stage manager (uncredited)
Richard Carle – Eunuch crowning Elmer (uncredited)
Louise Carver – Big German woman (uncredited)
Emile Chautard (uncredited)
Jackie Coogan – Himself, at premiere (uncredited)
Cecil B. DeMille – Himself (uncredited)
Drew Demorest – Larry's valet (uncredited)
Ann Dvorak – Chorus girl (uncredited)
Joseph Farnham – Himself (uncredited)
Pat Harmon – Doorman at premiere (uncredited)
Lottice Howell – Vocalist in "It Must Be You" (uncredited)
Arthur Lange – Himself, orchestral conductor (uncredited)
Theodore Lorch – Himself, dynamite scene director (uncredited)
Billy May – Himself (uncredited)
Doris McMahon – Singer and dancer in "Free and Easy" (uncredited)

Photographed by: Leonard Smith
Film editor: William LeVanway
Recording director: Douglas Shearer
Art director: Cedric Gibbons
Words and music by: Roy Turk, Fred E. Ahlert
Dances staged by: Sammy Lee
Production company: Metro-Goldwyn-Mayer
Distributed by: Metro-Goldwyn-Mayer

Elvira Plunkett wins a beauty contest that sees her on her way to Hollywood for an MGM screen test, accompanied by her formidable mother and less-than-formidable agent, Elmer J. Butts. On the train she meets and falls for Hollywood star Larry Mitchell. To cut a particularly long story short, Elmer and Ma Plunkett end up with movie contracts and Elvira ends up with Larry.

Being Buster's first talking role – he had appeared in the talkie *The Hollywood Revue of 1929*, but hadn't spoken – audiences were keen to hear his speaking voice. All was well, with the *New York Times* reporting on 19 April 1930 that "it is a pleasure to report that his voice in this vehicle, known as *Free and Easy*, thoroughly suits his unique personality".

Buster's first speaking performance also sees him perform a song and dance number in full clown make-up and garb, demonstrating the latest craze to hit the dance floor, the "Free and Easy".

MGM took the opportunity of loading the film, which was originally to be called *On the Set*, with a roster of studio names playing themselves, including directors Cecil B. DeMille, Fred Niblo and David Burton, and actors Jackie Coogan, Lionel Barrymore, William Haines and William Collier Sr.

At the same time as *Free and Easy* was being publicised, Buster was also lined up to appear in the film of *Lord Byron of Broadway*, which was originally to have starred William Haines and Bessie Love. Ultimately, like Haines and Love, Buster did not appear in the film – it's possible Cliff Edwards played the part that had been earmarked for him.

As with many early talkies, *Free and Easy* was remade in a foreign language version. Unlike other MGM stars, however, Buster appeared in variously the Spanish, French and German versions of some of his 1930s feature films himself, reading his lines phonetically off idiot boards – for an extra $12,500 per film. It was possibly easier for Buster than for most dramatic actors as, by the nature of his characters, he had fewer lines. It also saved the studio a lot of money – Buster surmised that this initially caused the studios to turn a blind eye to his drinking. Also, being obviously an American, and a comedian, the foreign audiences might assume that any mangling of the language was intended to be comical. *Free and Easy* was remade in Spanish as *Estrellados*, again directed by Edward Sedgwick and with Salvador de Alberich as uncredited dialogue director. This was the first feature production made by MGM that was entirely in Spanish. The intended meaning of the Spanish title is unclear. The usual translation is "Crashed", which is inaccurate and makes no sense.

Maybe the intention was to be reminiscent of "starry" ("*estrellado*"), or possibly something about fried eggs ("*huevos estrellados*") …

A French version, *Le metteur en scene* ("The Director"), was made by introducing English/French intertitles written by Alexander Stein and Allen Byre in place of the dialogue. This severely hampered the film's flow, with wordy sections being overrun by intertitles, and was deeply unpopular with Buster's legion of French fans when released there in 1931.

The AFI catalogue lists a silent version, at 5,240 feet.

It's reassuring to think that Buster may have been considering his own experience in making *Free and Easy* when delivering a line that's all the funnier for its incongruity – after a musical sequence towards the end of the film he hands a rifle to a chorus girl: "If the worst comes to the worst, save the last bullet for yourself." Oddly enough, this line also comes towards the end of Buster's next picture, *Doughboys*.

Doughboys

Aka *Forward March* (UK)

Directed by: Edward Sedgwick
Produced by: Buster Keaton
Presented by: Metro-Goldwyn-Mayer
Scenario by: Richard Schayer, Buster Keaton (uncredited)
Dialogue by: Al Boasberg, Richard Schayer
Story by: Al Boasberg, Sidney Lazarus, "The Big Shot"
Released: 30 August or 8 September 1930
Length: 81 minutes (9 reels, 7,325 feet)

Cast:
Buster Keaton – Elmer J. Stuyvesant Jr.
Sally Eilers – Mary
Cliff Edwards – Nescopeck
Edward Brophy – Sergeant Brophy
Victor Potel – Svendenburg
Arnold Korff – Gustave
Frank Mayo – Captain Scott
Pitzy Katz – Abie Cohn
William Steele – Lieutenant Randolph
Ann Dvorak – Chorus girl (scenes deleted)
Ann Sothern – Chorus girl (scenes deleted)
Bobby Barber – Doughboy (uncredited)

Sidney Bracey – Recruiter (uncredited)
John Carroll – Doughboy in Elmer's squad (uncredited)
Jack Cheatham – Guard house sentry (uncredited)
Jimmie Dundee – Riveter (uncredited)
Joseph W. Girard – General Hull (uncredited)
Pat Harmon – Induction non-com (uncredited)
Stanley J. Sandford – Recruit (uncredited)
Edward Sedgwick – Guggleheimer the camp cook (uncredited)
Harry Strang – Induction officer (uncredited)
Harry Stubbs – Sergeant (uncredited)

Photographed by: Leonard Smith
Film editor: William LeVanway
Recording director: Douglas Shearer
Art director: Cedric Gibbons
Words and music by: Edward Sedgwick, Joseph Meyer, Howard Johnson
Dances staged by: Sammy Lee
Production company: Metro-Goldwyn-Mayer
Distributed by: Metro-Goldwyn-Mayer

Aristocratic Elmer J. Stuyvesant Jr. is smitten with the young shop worker Mary, but she spurns his advances, and even offer of "a little dinner and a show", on the grounds that wealth shouldn't be able to buy a relationship. An understandable mix-up whereby Elmer mistakes an army recruitment office for a chauffeur employment agency sees him unwittingly enlist and sent to France. Happily Mary has also joined up as part of the entertainment division and is with Elmer. What's more, Elmer's selfless act of volunteering to fight for his country has softened her attitude towards him. Once in the trenches Elmer is unexpectedly reunited with his manservant from back home, Gustave, and a civilised end to hostilities definitely seems to be on the cards.

Buster's love of and prowess on the ukulele acted as a bond with Cliff Edwards (a.k.a. Ukulele Ike), and the pair became lifelong friends. The two made a number of comic 78s with Buster on ukulele and Edwards singing, though these were for private circulation of course and not for commercial distribution. Edwards would have a prominent role in Buster's next two features. He would be the voice of Jiminy Cricket in Disney's 1940 *Pinocchio*.

The soundtrack includes a rendition of the 1890s song "The Sidewalks of New York" by recruits in the canteen, a song that would also appear in Buster's next-but-one film, *Sidewalks of New York*.

The story is based in part on Buster's own experiences of putting on shows while in the army in France at the end of World War One, in particular his (what we might very loosely describe as) drag performance in the boisterous Apache dance routine.

Director Eddie Sedgwick plays the camp's cook, and also wrote the song "Military Man" sung by a group at the recruiting station.

The film, which had the tentative pre-production title of *War Babies*, was released as *Forward March* in the UK, and remade in a Spanish version, *¡De Frente, Marchen!*, also starring Buster, with Salvador de Alberich once again as dialogue director and released in December 1930. Interestingly, this version ran to 96 minutes, being some 1,300 feet longer. Both the German version and the French version (announced in March 1931, to be directed by Emile de Recat) were most probably simply dubbed versions of the original.

Parlor, Bedroom and Bath

Aka *Romeo in Pyjamas* (UK)

Directed by: Edward Sedgwick
Produced by: Buster Keaton
Presented by: Metro-Goldwyn-Mayer
Dialogue continuity by: Richard Schayer
Additional dialogue by: Robert E. Hopkins
From the play by: Charles W. Bell, Mark Swan
Released: 28 February 1931
Length: 73 minutes (8 reels)

Cast:
Buster Keaton – Reginald Irving
Charlotte Greenwood – Polly Hathaway
Reginald Denny – Jeffery Haywood
Cliff Edwards – Bell Hop
Dorothy Christy – Angelica Embrey
Joan Peers – Nita Leslie
Sally Eilers – Virginia Embrey
Natalie Moorhead – Leila Crofton
Edward Brophy – Detective
Walter Merrill – Frederick Leslie
Sidney Bracey – Butler
George Davis – Gardener (uncredited)
Tyrell Davis – Bertie (uncredited)

Photographed by: Leonard Smith
Film editor: William LeVanway
Recording director: Douglas Shearer
Art director: Cedric Gibbons
Production company: Metro-Goldwyn-Mayer
Distributed by: Metro-Goldwyn-Mayer

Virginia Embrey won't marry Jeffrey until her rather picky elder sister Angelica gets wed first. When shy Reggie Irving enters the Embrey household, by dint of being run over on a nearby lane, Jeffrey decides to pique Angelica's interest by building him up as a notorious womaniser. He enlists the help of his friend Polly to try to teach Reggie in the ways of the world.

The film could be a case of art imitating life, in that it had been reported that Buster had asked Natalie to marry him within of few weeks of their meeting, but she had refused on the grounds that she couldn't possibly marry before her younger sister Constance was safely wed. Constance married Greek tobacco importer John Pialoglou on Boxing Day 1920 (in a double wedding with Dorothy Gish). Natalie wrote to Buster in January 1921 that she was "alone now with Mother", and he should send for her if he was still up for it.

Exteriors for the film were shot at Buster's Italian villa in Beverly Hills, and show the lavish house and grounds that Buster had bought for Natalie.

Charlotte Greenwood played in the stage version on Broadway in 1917/18, and is in danger of stealing the film from Buster. She later had her own radio show on ABC and NBC. Metro first made the film in 1920 with Eugene Pallette and Ruth Stonehouse, directed by Edward Dillon.

The scene involving the breakdown of the Austin Bantam roadster on a railway track is straight from the climax of *One Week*. Buster argued that the lack of dialogue in the sequence proved that talking pictures didn't necessarily need continuous talk, but MGM weren't convinced.

German and French language versions were made – *Buster se Marie* ("Buster Gets Married"), directed by Claude Autant-Lara, and *Casanova wider Willen* ("A Reluctant Casanova"), directed by Edward Brophy, with Buster speaking his lines phonetically as usual. Actress Françoise Rosay appears in both films, though playing different parts.

Sidewalks of New York

Directed by: Jules White, Zion Myers
Produced by: Buster Keaton, Lawrence Weingarten (uncredited)
Presented by: Metro-Goldwyn-Mayer
Dialogue by: Robert E. Hopkins, Eric Hatch, Willard Mack (uncredited)
Story by: George Landy, Paul Gerard Smith
Released: 26 September 1931
Length: 74 minutes (8 reels)

Cast:
Buster Keaton – Harmon
Anita Page – Margie
Cliff Edwards – Poggle
Frank Rowan – Butch
Norman Phillips Jr. – Clipper
Frank LaRue – Sergeant
Oscar Apfel – Judge
Syd Saylor – Mulvaney
Clark Marshall – Lefty
Ann Brody – Tenement mother (uncredited)
Bobby Burns – Attorney (uncredited)
Monte Collins – James, Harmon's chauffeur (uncredited)
Drew Demorest – Dresser (uncredited)
Harry Strang – Cop (uncredited)
Jerry Tucker – Little boy sitting on curb (uncredited)
Dorothy Vernon – Tenement woman in window (uncredited)

Harry Wilson – One of Butch's henchmen (uncredited)
Robert Winkler – Little boy (uncredited)
Clifton Young – Street gang member (uncredited)

Photographed by: Leonard Smith
Film editor: Charles Hochberg, Basil Wrangell (uncredited)
Recording director: Douglas Shearer
Art director: Cedric Gibbons
Production company: Metro-Goldwyn-Mayer
Distributed by: Metro-Goldwyn-Mayer

Tenement block owner Homer Van Dine Harmon decides to do something to improve the lives of the kids in the lower East Side – a decision that is part philanthropy and part having just clapped eyes on Margie, the glamorous elder sister of Clipper, the leader of the young hoodlums. Even opening a well-equipped gym to harness the energy of the ne'er-do-wells doesn't quite get them on side. Clipper has the added problem of having to please local gangster Butch, who is grooming him for ever more nefarious activities. But when Harmon gets wind of Butch's life of crime, and Butch tells Clipper he has to finish off Harmon, it's a step too far.

Eddie Sedgwick was unavailable at the time of the shoot, and so the reins were passed to a couple of relatively inexperienced relative youngsters. Zion Myers and Jules White were at the time most noted for writing, directing, producing and starring in two-reelers featuring talking dogs – including the classics *So Quiet on the Canine Front* and *The Dogway Melody* – a genre that failed to appeal to Buster's sense of humour. They also treated Buster like one of their previous four-legged stars, taking it in turns to coach him in how to walk, stand and fall, making for a miserable experience for Buster, and contributing to him considering this to be his worst MGM picture. Which it really isn't.

The scheduled release date of 26 September was held back in parts of the US, including New York, as there were concerns over scenes in which the juveniles were being taught to steal. The censors had demanded that these scenes be "tightened up".

Jules White would again loom large in the Keaton story later in the decade, directing and/or producing all but one of the ten Columbia shorts that Buster made between 1939 and 1941.

Fourteen-year-old Norman Phillips Jr.'s father had died suddenly in February 1931, just three months before Buster offered him the part in *Sidewalks of New York*. Phillips Sr. had just been cast in Joan Crawford's *Laughing Sinners*.

A French version was reportedly made, again directed by Emile de Recat. The title was to be *Buster Millionaire*, although publicity for this release indicates that, like *Doughboys*, it was simply a French-dubbed version of the original. *Variety* reported that de Recat left MGM on 13 February 1932.

The Passionate Plumber

Directed by: Edward Sedgwick
Produced by: Buster Keaton, Harry Rapf
    (uncredited)
Presented by: Metro-Goldwyn-Mayer
Adaptation by: Laurence E. Johnson
Dialogue by: Ralph Spence
Released: 6 February 1932
Length: 73 minutes (8 reels)

Cast:
Buster Keaton – Elmer E. Tuttle
Jimmy Durante – Julius J. McCracken
Polly Moran – Albine
Irene Purcell – Patricia Jardine
Gilbert Roland – Tony Lagorce
Mona Maris – Nina Estrados
Maude Eburne – Aunt Charlotte
Henry Armetta – Bouncer
Paul Porcasi – Paul Le Maire
Jean Del Val – Chauffeur
August Tollaire – General Bouschay
Edward Brophy – Man outside beauty
    parlour (uncredited)
Heinie Conklin – Hunter with rifle at duel (uncredited)
Carl M. Leviness – Casino patron (uncredited)
Fred Malatesta – Tony's second (uncredited)
Rolfe Sedan – Tony's second (uncredited)
Stanhope Wheatcroft – Casino patron (uncredited)
Florence Wix – Casino patron (uncredited)

Photographed by: Norbert Brodine
Film editor: William S. Gray
Recording director: Douglas Shearer
Production company: Metro-Goldwyn-Mayer
Distributed by: Metro-Goldwyn-Mayer

Elmer, an American in Paris, and a plumber to boot, is summoned by chauffeur Julius to fix the shower of rich socialite Patricia. She is unsure of her feelings for caddish Tony. "But I love him. I despise him. I despise myself for loving him." Finding Elmer in Patricia's shower, Tony challenges him to duel, which ends well for all, but with the added complication of Patricia's feelings for Elmer becoming apparent. To keep Tony at bay, Patricia plays up her relationship with Elmer – although Patricia being Patricia, there's often not a lot of playing up to do. And while all this is going on, Tony is also wooing tempestuous Nina, who has the unfortunate habit of throwing anything breakable in the general direction of his head. Extensive farce finally resolves the love rectangle, with the maid in the arms of the chauffeur for good measure.

The Passionate Plumber is based on *The Cardboard Lover*, a 1928 silent comedy which itself is based on a translation by Valerie Wyngate and P.G. Wodehouse of Jacques Deval's play *Dans sa cadeur naïve* ("In his naïve candour"). Tallulah Bankhead had played the lead in the original West End production. Buster's part was played on stage by Leslie Howard.

Early reports had Robert Montgomery as the lead, although MGM soon announced that Buster would star. Charlotte Greenwood was also mentioned as a cast member, but she isn't in the film. Swedish actor Nils Asther was initially announced as a member of the cast, and indeed is mentioned in production reports in the press as late as January 1932, yet he also doesn't appear. It is possible that there was confusion over the fact that he had starred in the original 1928 version of the film. Asther went on to play General Yen in Frank Capra's *The Bitter Tea of General Yen*.

It was the first of three films in which Buster was paired with Jimmy Durante. The incongruous partnership was not a success, as Buster sensed from the off that there was little comic chemistry between the two, and his own silent strength was lost against Durante's motormouth delivery. In fact, reports during filming suggested that Buster was sensitive to the difference in styles, "leaning backwards" so as not to eclipse Durante and even suggesting retakes where he felt Durante was overshadowed. Nevertheless, the two got on well off screen and became friends, remaining on good terms over the years.

The first set-piece of Buster-in-the-bathroom leading to the duel was remade in 1941 as *She's Oil Mine*.

One scene features a rather infamous shot in which a Paris hotel balcony overlooks the ocean.

The film was remade in French as *Le Plombier Amoureux*, directed by Claude Autant-Lara, with Buster again putting in a phonetic performance. It would be the last foreign language remake of one of his films. Future foreign language versions were made by dubbing the dialogue, with varying degrees of success.

Speak Easily

Directed by: Edward Sedgwick
Produced by: Buster Keaton
Presented by: Metro-Goldwyn-Mayer
Dialogue continuity by: Ralph Spence, Laurence E. Johnson
From the story by: Clarence Budington Kelland
Released: 13 August 1932
Length: 80 minutes (9 reels)

Cast:
Buster Keaton – Professor Post
Jimmy Durante – James Dodge
Ruth Selwyn – Pansy Peets
Thelma Todd – Eleanor Espere
Hedda Hopper – Mrs. Peets
William Pawley – Griffo
Sidney Toler – Stage director
Lawrence Grant – Dr. Bolton
Henry Armetta – Tony
Edward Brophy – Reno
Oscar Apfel – Lawyer's representative (uncredited)
Reginald Barlow – Billington (uncredited)
Jack Baxley – Tom, Sheriff's deputy (uncredited)
Sidney Bracey – Jenkins (uncredited)
Jim Farley – Station agent (uncredited)
DeWitt Jennings – Sheriff of Lincoln County (uncredited)
Fred Kelsey – Process server (uncredited)
Dave O'Brien – Chorus boy (uncredited)
Inez Palange – Rosa, Tony's wife (uncredited)
Harry Tenbrook – Baggage man (uncredited)

Photographed by: Harold Wenstrom
Film editor: William LeVanway
Recording director: Douglas Shearer
Art director: Cedric Gibbons
Music by: William Axt (uncredited)
Production company: Metro-Goldwyn-Mayer
Distributed by: Metro-Goldwyn-Mayer

Shy Professor Timolean Zanders Post's quiet life takes a different turn when his assistant, in an attempt to make him get out and see the world, fakes a letter saying he has inherited $750,000. En route to getting out and seeing New York, Post encounters the Midnight Maid Company, a troupe of decidedly amateur players led by Jimmy Dodge, and more specifically becomes infatuated with dancer Pansy Peets. When debts threaten to kill the show, the learned Professor offers to finance the production, suggesting elements of Greek dance be introduced. Meanwhile, scheming Eleanor Espere plays on Post's naivety and good nature in an attempt to gain influence and money. Opening night in New York sees the production descend into farce due to the Professor's well-meant intervention. But this farce is a hit farce, and the fictional inheritance becomes irrelevant when Post sells half of his stake in the show to a producer for a genuine $100,000.

The film is based on "Footlights", a *Saturday Evening Post* story by Clarence Budington Kelland, which MGM and RKO were competing to acquire.

The screenplay includes a variation on one of Buster's favourite routines, that of putting an inebriated woman to bed.

Whether error or coincidence, the first shot establishes "Potts College, Founded AD. MDCCCLXXVI", whereas Buster's character is called Post.

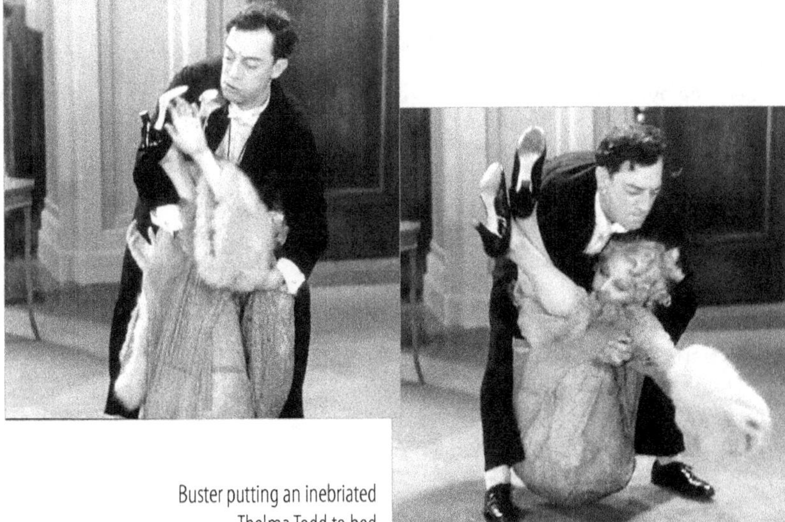

Buster putting an inebriated
Thelma Todd to bed

Buster felt it was Durante's best of the three films they made together, partly because the character he played was much like the real Durante. With this film, Buster got wind of the fact that MGM were building Durante up at Buster's expense. Whether this was true or not, it irked Buster, who felt he was a fixture at the studio and wasn't ready to be cast aside.

Nevertheless *Variety* reported that as Buster and Durante began shooting *Speak Easily*, the studio "intends teaming the pair permanently".

The film heavily features the song "Good Times Are Here Again", with lyrics by MGM story department head Sam Marx.

Shooting took place in May and June of 1932. Buster's personal problems, compounded by his drinking, meant that 11 shooting days were lost, costing MGM $33,000 out of a total production cost of $420,000. In July, Buster's contract with MGM was renewed and included a clause having 20% of his $3,000-a-week salary withheld until these losses were repaid.

With filming complete the next project being spoken of was to team Buster and Durante with Jackie Coogan in *Be Your Age*, although nothing concrete came of it. It was not the last time the three names would be linked, however.

What! No Beer?

Directed by: Edward Sedgwick
Produced by: Lawrence Weingarten (uncredited)
Presented by: Metro-Goldwyn-Mayer
Original story by: Robert E. Hopkins
Screenplay by: Carey Wilson
Additional dialogue by: Jack Cluett
Released: 10 February 1933
Length: 65 minutes (7 reels)

Cast:
Buster Keaton – Elmer J. Butts
Jimmy Durante – Jimmy Potts
Roscoe Ates – Schultz
Phyllis Barry – Hortense
John Miljan – Butch Lorado
Henry Armetta – Tony
Edward Brophy – Spike Moran
Charles Dunbar – Mulligan
Charles Giblyn – Chief
Sidney Bracey – Dr. Smith (uncredited)

Eddy Chandler – Cop (uncredited)
James Donlan – Al (uncredited)
Billy Engle – Beer drinker (uncredited)
Sherry Hall – Moran's henchman (uncredited)
Pat Harmon – Moran's henchman (uncredited)
George Irving – Politician (uncredited)
Al Jackson – Stool pigeon (uncredited)
Wilbur Mack – Banker Jordan (uncredited)
Broderick O'Farrell – Police chemist (uncredited)
Lee Phelps – Passer-by (uncredited)
Rolfe Sedan – Barber (uncredited)
Harry Tenbrook – Moran's henchman (uncredited)

Cinematography: Harold Wenstrom
Edited by: Frank Sullivan
Sound by: Douglas Shearer
Production company: Metro-Goldwyn-Mayer
Distributed by: Metro-Goldwyn-Mayer

The end of Prohibition is nigh. Good news for barber Jimmy, who persuades taxidermist Elmer to invest his life savings in buying a brewery. But less good news for rival bootleggers Spike Moran and Butch Lorado, and particularly for Butch's moll Hortense, who sees her dreams of owning a Rolls Royce town car recede yet further. When Hortense, playing on Elmer's infatuation with her, learns that Spike has cut a deal with Jimmy and Elmer, a gang war breaks out between the rival black marketeers, with the brewsome twosome caught in the crossfire.

There appear to be three cuts of the film, lengths of 65, 70 and 78 minutes are listed in the American Film Institute catalogue. The currently available standard cut is 65 minutes, but the contemporary review in *Motion Picture Herald*, for example, gives a length of 78 minutes. A preview on 3 February reported the film running at 86 minutes which, if correct, suggests substantial cuts were made. An early review in *The Hollywood Reporter* on 31 January warns "The picture needs plenty of trimming – which it will undoubtedly get – to bring the laughs closer together." Shooting reportedly finished on 28 January, just two weeks before the film's official release. The title had only been decided upon the previous week.

Roscoe Ates, billed here as Rosco Ates as he often was in his early films, was a former vaudeville performer known in films for his stutter. He had appeared in *Freaks* in 1931.

The film shows that Buster is clearly in no position to work – Natalie had been given an interlocutory decree of divorce and had custody of Jimmy and Bobby, and Buster was drinking over a bottle of whiskey a day. He is physically out of condition and his speech and reactions are sluggish and slow. The film, burdened with a pretty dire script, was to become an acute embarrassment to him. His only contribution was the cascade of beer barrels chasing him down a hill, lifted from the rock avalanche scene in *Seven Chances*.

Studio head Louis B. Mayer's impatience with Buster's problems finally reached breaking point a week before the film opened. Clearly not averse to kicking a man when he was down, Mayer wrote to Buster to tell him that his contract had been terminated, even though a new project, *Buddies* with Durante and Jackie Coogan, was already lined up and pre-publicity had started. Press reports presented an alternative reality. They stated that Buster had asked to be released from the contract he had signed with MGM the previous October, unhappy with having to relinquish top billing and to split the credit with his co-star (he and Durante had equal billing in *What! No Beer?*).

And so 1933 was decidedly Buster's *annus horribilis*, his peremptory sacking on 2 February, on the release of arguably his worst film to date, came just after his disastrous "marriage of inconvenience" to Mae Scriven (of which he remembered nothing, being caught in a cycle of alcohol binges and periods in shady sanatoriums at the time) and shortly before the untimely death of his dear friend and mentor Roscoe Arbuckle.

As a postscript, maybe Buster's year can best be summed up by an astonishing paragraph tucked away in *Variety* of 21 November 1933:

> Buster Keaton saved from death by being dragged out of a small volcano into which he fell while hunting alone near Mexicali. Two Mexicans heard his yells and pulled him out with clothes singed by sulphur.

Grand Mills Hotel – The One That Got Away

An intriguing film that might have been.

In an effort to gain control of his life and wrest control of his career from MGM, a temporarily sober Buster pitched an idea for a story to MGM producer Irving Thalberg.

MGM's all-star *Grand Hotel* had just been completed and would go on to win the Oscar for Best Picture of 1932. (And incidentally earn the distinction of being the only film to win Best Picture Oscar but not receive a single nomination in any other category.) It concerns the interconnected fates of guests at Berlin's high class Grand Hotel. The comings and goings are observed by permanent resident Dr. Otternschlag, played by Lewis Stone, a disfigured veteran of World War I.

Lionel Barrymore plays accountant Otto Kringelein, who is dying of consumption and is spending his final days in the lap of luxury. His former boss, the tyrannical womanising Preysing, played by Wallace Beery, is also in the hotel trying to negotiate a high-level business merger. He hires wannabe actress and erstwhile floozy Flaemmchen (Joan Crawford) as a secretary to assist him.

Serial card sharp and occasional jewel thief Baron von Geigern is played by John Barrymore and Greta Garbo is the weary, fading Russian ballerina Grusinskaya, who wants to be alone. When the ballerina catches the Baron in her room attempting to steal her jewellery, she inevitably falls for his charms.

The subsequent intrigue, philandering and murder go unnoticed by Dr. Otternschlag, who laments as the film ends that things in the hotel are "Always the same … Nothing ever happens."

Buster's parody was to be set in New York's real life Mills Hotel in the Bowery, a municipal refuge for bums and near-bums. Buster would play Lionel Barrymore's part, but dying of hiccups having been given only 30 to 40 years to live. "Only 30 to 40 years? That means I must not lose a single moment." Playing the power-mad factory boss would be Oliver Hardy, manufacturer of front collar buttons, trying to effect a merger with Stan Laurel, manufacturer of back collar buttons. He would have an affair with the brash, loud-mouthed, knock-about comedienne Polly Moran – the female lead in *The Passionate Plumber* – playing Flaemmchen.

Garbo's part would go to robust 64 year-old Marie Dressler. Buster imagined her opening scene: "She would look into the full-length mirror, open her ankle-length ermine robe, exposing her battleship of a figure in ballet dancer's costume with slippers about a foot and half long and murmur, 'I think I am getting too old to dance, and I fear that my public doesn't want me any more.'" Her love interest, the bogus Count, was to be played by Jimmy Durante.

The whole goings on are observed by Edward Everett Horton as the war veteran, here wearing a Band Aid having cut himself shaving.

Thalberg agreed to give the idea some thought and get back to Buster. Unfortunately, in the meantime Buster was fired by Thalberg's boss Louis B. Mayer, and worse still was in the throes of horrific alcohol withdrawal when his friend Eddie Sedgwick tracked him down to tell him that Thalberg had squared it with Mayer and the film could go ahead. Buster, sick with withdrawal symptoms and still boiling with rage and grief, told Sedgwick, "Tell the goddamned bastard to go to hell."

THE EDUCATIONAL FILMS SHORTS

The Gold Ghost

Directed by: Charles Lamont, Buster Keaton (uncredited)
Produced by: E.H. Allen
Presented by: E.W. Hammons
Story by: Ewart Adamson, Nick Barrows
Adaptation and continuity by: Ernest Pagano, Charles Lamont
Released: 16 March 1934
Length: 21 minutes (2 reels)

Cast:
Buster Keaton – Wattie
Warren Hymer – "Bugs" Kelly
Dorothy Dix – Gloria
Joe Young – Pat
William Worthington – Jim, Gloria's father
Lloyd Ingraham – George, Wattie's father
Leo Willis – Claim jumper
Billy Engle – Short miner (uncredited)
Al Thompson – Miner (uncredited)

Photographed by: Dwight Warren   Sound by: Karl Zint
Production company: Educational Films Corporation
Distributed by: Fox Film Corporation

Wattie (or is it Waddy?) overhears his sweetheart Gloria tell her father she wants nothing to do with him until he proves himself to be a man. Wanting to be alone, he takes a drive from Boston to the ghost town of Vulture City, Nevada. The lack of people, especially women, suits him fine and, finding the sheriff's discarded badge, he puts it on. He strikes up an unlikely friendship with gangster pilot "Bugs" Kelly, who has just crashed landed nearby. When gold is discovered, ghost town turns to boom town, bringing Gloria with the crowds. Time for the sheriff to prove himself.

Some months after completing *What! No Beer?*, Buster signed up with a new production company, Kennedy Sunshine Specials, based in Florida. Shooting began on *The Fisherman*, directed by Marshall Neilan and written by Buster's old colleague Lew Lipton. However, the company soon folded, although not before Buster had pocketed $27,000 for his trouble.

As no offers were then coming his way from the major studios, Buster took the advice of his friend screen-writer Ernest Pagano to throw his lot in with an independent studio. So in January 1934, he signed with Educational Pictures on a contract for $5,000 per film, six films per year. The reputation of Educational Pictures, like Buster's career, had gone from a high in the 1920s to a low ebb, and shorts were churned out in three to five days on a budget of around $20,000. Buster would make sixteen two-reelers with Educational Pictures before the company dissolved after Twentieth Century-Fox withdrew its support in 1937. Bob Hope began his career with Educational – his debut picture *Going Spanish* was released a fortnight before *The Gold Ghost*.

Buster's first Educational Pictures short was written with Pagano, and began shooting on 14 February. Its release just a month later gives an idea of the breakneck speed at which these shorts were churned out. A mere three days were typically put aside for filming.

Educational Pictures had just developed a new, cheap way of making trick stills by placing a sheet of glass at an angle in front of the camera to catch the reflection of an offstage scene and giving a ghost-like double image. This device was described in *The Hollywood Reporter* as being first used by the studio on Buster's short – for the fantasy sequence half way through when Buster has a gunfight in a deserted saloon.

Buster's sister Louise had also signed with Educational Pictures in November 1933, so it was only a matter of time before he would once again appear on screen with a fellow Keaton or three.

Joe Young is the brother of the better-known Robert. He later acted under the name of Roger Moore.

The Gold Ghost was initially tentatively called *Crowded Out*. It was well received, with *Variety* executing a text-book back-handed compliment, "Buster Keaton

is almost a forgotten story, but if he can turn out more shorts as consistently funny as this one, he doesn't have to reach for a back seat."

Allez Oop!

Directed by: Charles Lamont, Buster Keaton (uncredited)
Produced by: E.H. Allen
Presented by: E.W. Hammons
Story by: Ernest Pagano, Ewart Adamson
Released: May 1934
Length: 21 minutes (2 reels)

Cast:
Buster Keaton – Elmer
Dorothy Sebastian – Paula Stevens
George Lewis – Apollo the Wonderful
Harry Myers – Circus spectator
The Flying Escalantes – Themselves
Leonard Kibrick – Boy watching Buster (uncredited)

Photographed by: Dwight Warren
Sound by: Karl Zint
Production company: Educational Films Corporation
Distributed by: Fox Film Corporation

> Watch repairer Elmer is given two tickets for the circus in exchange for advertising the event in his shop. He takes along a new customer, Paula Stevens, but only succeeds in bringing her together with trapeze artist Apollo the Wonderful. He resolves to beat Apollo at his own game, but his laboured attempts to teach himself trapeze techniques in his back garden seem unpromising. However, when Paula needs to be rescued from her second floor apartment, maybe his hard work will pay off.

Filming began on 25 April 1934, again leaving just a month for shooting, developing, editing, production and distribution before the film's release.

The Flying Escalantes make their second appearance in a Buster Keaton short, having also appeared in *Neighbors* in 1920. The group were friends of Buster from his vaudeville days.

Dorothy Sebastian appears with Buster for the third and final time, four years after their affair had ended and she had married William Boyd. By 1936 her marriage had ended and she eventually took up with Buster again. The story goes that when Buster met Eleanor, the two of them hatched a plan to introduce Dorothy to a handsome wrestler from the Hollywood Legion Stadium in the hope that they would hit it off. The plan worked, they did, and Buster felt able to marry Eleanor with a clear conscience.

According to *The Hollywood Reporter* of 17 May 1934, the deadpan comic Cully Richards was signed by Sam Goldwyn to appear in *Barbary Coast* in "the role originally intended for Buster Keaton". It is unlikely that it was Buster's choice not to appear in the film, but in the event Goldwyn suspended production in protest against the over-zealous censorship that was starting at the time, and Cully Richards does not appear in the finished film anyway.

On 3 August 1934, *Motion Picture Daily* reported that Buster had been signed by producer Hal Roach for a part in a film called *Greek is Greek*. This was to have been a two-reeler, but no film of that title was made.

Le Roi des Champs-Élysées

Directed by: Max Nosseck
Produced by: Seymour Nebenzal
Presented by: Nero Film
Scenario by: Arnold Lipp
Dialogue by: Yves Mirande
Released: 11 December 1934
Length: 70 minutes (7 reels)

Cast:
Buster Keaton – Buster Garner / Jim le Balafré
Paulette Dubost – Germaine
Madeleine Guitty – Madame Garner
|Lucien] **Callamand**
[Jacques] **Dumesnil** – Gangster
[Pierre] **Piérade**
[Gaston] **Dupray** – Director
[Raymond] **Blot**
Colette Darfeuil – Simone
Paul Clerget (uncredited)
Jim Gérald (uncredited)
Franck Maurice (uncredited)
Henry Prestat (uncredited)

Cinematography: Robert Le Febvre
Edited by: Jean Delannoy (uncredited)
Music by: Joe Hajos
Production company: Nero Film
Distributed in France by: S.A.F. Paramount

> Buster is fired from his job of giving out flyers in the form of fake 1,000 franc notes having accidentally given away genuine notes. Seeking solace with his mother who is a prompter at the local theatre, he manages to wreak havoc and sabotage a production. He decides life has nothing for him, but before he can end it all he spots a beautiful girl he has loved from afar and discovers life does have something after all. He gets the role of a prisoner in the play "Le Roi des Champs-Élysées". But confusion taps on the window when his doppelganger, a gangster, breaks out of jail and our man is whisked off to the gangsters' hideout as the returning hero. He lures the hoods to the theatre so that the showdown is played out before a paying audience.

Although Buster appears to have had no hand in the writing of the screenplay, there are echoes of many of his earlier pictures. The serial suicide attempts in *Hard Luck*, the sabotaging of the stage play in *Speak Easily* (and others), and the mistaken identity of *The Goat* (and in fact *Convict 13*) all come to mind.

Filming started on 3 August 1934 at Joinville Studios on the outskirts of Paris, with Margot Films, who pulled out due to financial problems. In all, the film was shot in just 12 days. It was not successful and, despite Paramount being slated to distribute the film, it failed to get a US release.

As was not uncommon with French films, most of the cast are credited only by their surnames.

Buster takes on the double role rather well, but the film is let down by Buster (both of them) being dubbed terribly – apart from two lines towards the end, "Vive le chef!" and "Ouvre la porte", which are clearly him. The garish soundtrack and occasionally sped up action also don't help.

Footage from the climax of an earlier Nero film, Fritz Lang's *The Testament of Dr. Mabuse* from 1933, is used in the final car chase scene.

The final shot is of Buster smiling as he (*spoiler alert*) gets the girl – a closing gimmick he wisely never used before or since (despite the near miss in *Steamboat Bill, Jr.*). The studio misguidedly thought this would be box office draw, and broadcast the fact that a grinning Buster was part of his contract. The public clearly thought otherwise and stayed away in droves – *Variety* reported "a moderate amount of whistling and booing from the audience" at the French premiere. (In notable contrast, MGM's "Garbo Laughs" tag for *Ninotchka* would be hugely successful five years down the line.)

Palooka from Paducah

Aka *Weight for It* (UK)

Directed by: Charles Lamont
Produced by: E.H. Allen
Presented by: E.W. Hammons
Story by: Glen Lambert
Released: 11 January 1935
Length: 20 minutes (2 reels)

Cast:
Buster Keaton – Jim Diltz
Myra Keaton – Ma Diltz
Joe Keaton – Pa Diltz
Louise Keaton – Sis Diltz
Dewey Robinson – Elmer Diltz
Bull Montana – "Bullfrog" Kraus

Photographed by: Dwight Warren
Sound by: Karl Zint
Production company: Educational Films Corporation
Distributed by: Fox Film Corporation

The Diltz family being in constant financial straits, when Pa hears there's money to be made in wrestling he decides that Elmer is the Diltz to earn it. As Elmer prepares to fight "Bullfrog" Kraus, Ma asks Jim to look out for his brother. He assures her that anyone who harms one hair of the boy's beard will have to answer to him. But when Jim tries to protect Elmer in the ring, "Bullfrog" turns on him, firing Elmer up to the extent that, with the help of Ma, he gains the upper hand.

Although Buster played a character called Elmer on 17 occasions, here Elmer is his brother – the only member of the family not played by a Keaton.

The usual musical theme introducing Buster's shorts is replaced here by vocal quartet singing a country tune, just to get us in the mood.

The Four Keatons
with
Dewey Robinson

Unfortunately Joe's performance shows clear signs of his suffering with alcoholism. This would be his last film and therefore the last appearance on film of The Three Keatons (plus Louise). Despite the obvious on-screen rapport between the many Keatons, this is one of Buster's weaker Educational shorts.

This was filmed after Buster had taken a break from his series of Educational shorts to make a couple of low-budget features – travelling to France to appear in *Le Roi des Champs-Élysées* and then on to England to film *The Invader* (although this was not released until 1936).

One Run Elmer

Directed by: Charles Lamont
Produced by: E.H. Allen
Presented by: E.W. Hammons
Story by: Glen Lambert
Released: 22 February 1935
Length: 19 minutes (2 reels, 1,753 feet)

Cast:
Buster Keaton – Elmer
Lona André – Molly
Dewey Robinson – The umpire
Harold Goodwin – Jim
Bobby Dunn – Ball player (uncredited)

Al Thompson – Truck driver (uncredited)
Jim Thorpe – Second baseman (uncredited)
Jack Shutta (unconfirmed)

Photographed by: Dwight Warren
Sound by: Frank Grenzbach
Production company: Educational Films Corporation
Distributed by: Fox Film Corporation

> Business is slow at Elmer's De Luxe gas station on a dirt road 2372 miles from New York and 561⅔ miles from Los Angeles. But rivalry kicks in when Jim's Super De Luxe gas station opens opposite. A passing motorist tells the pair she is a baseball fan, prompting the rivals to take positions in opposing local teams. The victor will win the hand of the girl.

Filming in the Californian desert was held up for two days due to a rainstorm, during which Buster took the opportunity to have a drink or several. Meaning an extra day was lost to a hangover. Nevertheless, his performance is assured throughout the film. The comparative lack of dialogue will also have suited Buster.

Many of the gags used in the baseball match were ones Buster developed for the charity games he helped to arrange.

Lona André – credited here with the accent on the e – was a keen golfer and in 1938 allegedly held a world record for speed in women's golf by playing 156 holes in just under 12 hours.

Jim Thorpe won gold medals for both pentathlon and decathlon at the 1912 Olympics in Stockholm, the first Native American to win gold for the US.

Hayseed Romance

Directed by: Charles Lamont
Produced by: E.H. Allen
Presented by: E.W. Hammons
Written by: Charles Lamont
Dialogue and continuity by: Glen Lambert
Released: 15 March 1935
Length: 20 minutes (2 reels)

Cast:
Buster Keaton – Elmer Dolittle
Jane Jones – Miss Green, Molly's aunt
Dorothea Kent – Molly
Robert McKenzie – Justice of the Peace (uncredited)

Photographed by: Dwight Warren
Sound by: Karl Zint
Production company: Educational Films Corporation
Distributed by: Fox Film Corporation

Elmer answers an ad – "Wanted: Young man, intelligent and alert, to make himself useful on farm; object matrimony". He is disappointed when the young girl he meets at the farm turns out to be the niece of the battleaxe who has placed the ad. Nonetheless he knuckles down to making himself useful but inevitably creates more chaos than order. His conscience persuades him to leave the farm and the girl, but the tables are turned when a shotgun wedding takes an unexpected turn.

This was the first of two shorts loosely referencing an earlier film – here it is the forbidding domestic aspects of *My Wife's Relations*.

Jane Jones was mostly cast as a singer – in *Barbary Coast*, *Alexander's Ragtime Band* and *The Roaring Twenties*, for example – and here she is perfect for her destructive turn at the piano. Her distinctive size makes it rather apparent when a stunt double is used, the person in question being about a third the size of Ms Jones.

The picture's working title was *Matrimony Lane*.

Tars and Stripes

Directed by: Charles Lamont
Produced by: E.H. Allen
Presented by: E.W. Hammons
Story by: Charles Lamont
Adaptation by: Ewart Adamson
Released: 3 May 1935
Length: 20 minutes (2 reels, 1,830 feet)

Cast:
Buster Keaton – Apprentice Seaman Elmer Dolittle
Vernon Dent – Chief Gunners Mate Richard Mack
Dorothea Kent – Mack's girlfriend
Jack Shutta – Officer
William Lewis– Sailor (uncredited)
Al Thompson– Sailor (uncredited)
Bert Young– Sailor (uncredited)

Photographed by: Dwight Warren
Sound by: Hugo Grenzbach
Production company: Educational Films Corporation
Distributed by: Fox Film Corporation

Apprentice Seaman Elmer Dolittle is struggling at the Naval Training Station, and more often than not finds himself in the brig. Nevertheless, Chief Gunners Mate Richard Mack is intent on making a sailor out of him. To add to Elmer's problems, Mack's girlfriend takes a shine to him after he helps her with a broken heel.

The film was shot in March 1934 at the San Diego Naval Training Station. In April it was announced that Educational was closing production of films in Hollywood to concentrate on producing two-reelers in New York under the stewardship of Al Christie.

The plot seems to be a nod towards aspects of *Doughboys*, with Vernon Dent and Dorothea Kent taking the Ed Brophy and Sally Eilers parts.

In what was presumably intended as a reference to an aspect of Buster's silent career that didn't exist, custard pies feature briefly in a spurious scene.

The E-Flat Man

Directed by: Charles Lamont
Produced by: E.H. Allen
Presented by: E.W. Hammons
Story by: Glen Lambert, Charles Lamont
Released: 9 August 1935
Length: 20 minutes (2 reels)

Cast:
Buster Keaton – Elmer
Dorothea Kent – Elmer's girl
Broderick O'Farrell – Mr. Reynolds, Police Sergeant
Charles McAvoy – Hoodlum
Si Jenks – Farmer
Fern Emmett – Farmer's wife
Jack Shutta – Policeman

Matthew Betz – Hood with toothache (uncredited)
Bud Jamison – Cop (uncredited)

Photographed by: Dwight Warren
Sound by: Karl Zint
Production company: Educational Films Corporation
Distributed by: Fox Film Corporation

A drugstore robbery takes place while Elmer is attempting to elope from the neighbouring building with his sweetheart. When the police arrive, the robbers take off in Elmer's car, leaving Elmer to inadvertently commandeer the police car. Alerted to the mix-up by the police radio, they abandon the car and spend the night in a haystack. Next morning, a farmer offers them food in exchange for labour, but a radio APB sees them on the run again. After a night in a refrigerated railway wagon, it seems there's nothing for it but to give themselves up to the police.

This was Buster's first film under a new contract with Educational Pictures.

Fern Emmett would also appear with Buster in *Three on a Limb*. An extraordinarily hard working character actress, she appeared in some 244 films in her 20-year career, including 29 with her husband Henry Roquemore.

Si Jenks, who plays the grizzly old farmer, would play alongside Buster in a similar role in *God's Country* in 1946.

The Timid Young Man

Directed by: Mack Sennett
Produced by: Mack Sennett
Presented by: E.W. Hammons
Written by: Glen Lambert, Charles Lamont (uncredited)
Released: 25 October 1935
Length: 20 minutes (2 reels, 1,786 feet)

Cast:
Buster Keaton – Milton
Lona Andre – Helen
Stanley J. Sandford – Mortimer
Kitty McHugh – Milton's fiancée

Harry Bowen – Milton's valet
Don Brodie – Desk clerk (uncredited)
James C. Morton – Helen's father (uncredited)

Photographed by: Dwight Warren
Sound by: Karl Zint
Production company: Educational Films Corporation
Distributed by: Twentieth Century-Fox Film Corporation

> To escape from a marriage he finds himself embroiled in, Milton heads for the mountains. On the way he picks up Helen, who's pretty much in the same position. Both of them make it clear that they hate the opposite sex. On the way they run a driver, Mortimer, off the road, who follows them into the hills and latches onto them at their camp. Hot on his heels is Milton's would-be bride. While she gets physical with Mortimer, and not in a good way, Helen and Milton make their getaway, both still expressing hatred of the opposite sex.

The Timid Young Man is the only film on which Buster and Mack Sennett worked together. In his somewhat uneven autobiography, *King of Comedy*, Sennett lists Buster among the many stars whose careers he built up. For his part Buster boasted that there's one person who never worked for Sennett: "That's me, Buster Keaton".

Stanley J. ("Tiny") Sandford was a staple of Laurel and Hardy films, and had appeared with Buster in *Doughboys*. Kitty McHugh is the sister of character actors Matt (who appeared in a couple of Buster's Columbia shorts) and Frank.

Shortly before or after Buster was filming *The Timid Young Man*, his mother Myra and sister Louise shot *Way Up Thar*, also directed by Mack Sennett for Educational Pictures. This film is notable for being Sennett's last film, for being 1940s star Joan Davis's first film, and for featuring a 24-year-old Roy Rogers (billed as Leonard Slye) as a band member.

In early October 1935, shortly before the release of the film, *Variety* reported that Buster was in hospital in a serious condition with a nervous breakdown, following his divorce from Mae Scriven "on charges of cruelty". Buster had of course been on a bender following the divorce – Mae had taken half his possessions including his beloved St Bernard, Elmer, and when Buster tried to find the dog, he discovered that she had sold him. While in hospital he was told that if he continued to drink it would probably kill him. On his release from hospital he went to his club, drank two Manhattans, and pretty much stayed off the booze for the next five years.

The Invader

Aka *An Old Spanish Custom* (US)

Directed by: Adrian Brunel
Produced by: Harold Richman, Sam Spiegel
Presented by: J.H. Hoffberg
Script by: Edwin Greenwood, Buster Keaton (uncredited)
Released: 2 January 1936
Length: 61 minutes (6 reels)

Cast:
Buster Keaton – Leander Proudfoot
Lupita Tovar – Lupita Melez
Esme Percy – Jose
Lyn Harding – Gonzalo Gonzalez
Andreas Malandrinos – Carlos the barman
Hilda Moreno – Carmita
Clifford Heatherley – David Cheeseman
Webster Booth – Cantina singer

Cinematography: Eugen Schuefftan, Eric L. Gross
Editor: Daniel Birt, Rudi Fehr (uncredited)
Sound: Denis Scanlan
Musical director: John Greenwood
Production company: British & Continental
Distributed by: J.H. Hoffberg, Metro-Goldwyn-Mayer

The yacht *Invader* docks at a southern Spanish town bringing wealthy Leander Proudfoot ("the sort of boob who goes on the stage when the magician wants someone"). He stumbles into a love polygon involving bar owner Gonzalo, exotic dancer Lupita, and lothario Jose ("in love with himself, without a rival"). Lupita's plan to make Gonzalo jealous by flirting with the Americano, and so leaving the way clear for Jose, runs into a spot of bother when she can't help fallin' in love with the hapless Leander. The situation can only be settled by a three-way duel.

While he was shooting *Le Roi des Champs-Élysées* in Paris in 1934, Buster was contacted by Sam Spiegel and offered $12,000 to go to England to appear in *The Invader*. Filming started at Worton Hall Studios in September 1934.

The film was based on Buster's own story outline and he wrote most of the gags, although he received no writing credit. Unfortunately, despite some delicious Keatonesque moments and understated offhand gags, the film is torpedoed by a lack of money and curiously lacklustre direction by Adrian Brunel.

Sam Spiegel later moved to Hollywood and produced such classics as *The African Queen*, *The Bridge on the River Kwai* and *Lawrence of Arabia*. Meanwhile, British & Continental Films went into voluntary liquidation in April 1935.

The cinematographer, credited as Eric L. Gross, was Eric Cross.

The film was remade in 1939 as *Pest from the West*, Buster's first Columbia short, and shows the potential value of two-reelers in tightening up over-extended feature films. The ending of *The Invader* drags on somewhat, certainly compared to the snappy conclusion to *Pest from the West*.

It was filmed at an unhappy time for Buster – the Inland Revenue was suing him for $28,000 in back taxes and he was forced to declare himself bankrupt. The following year, his second wife Mae Scriven sued for divorce, naming a certain Leah Clampitt Sewell (I kid you not) in a $200,000 loss of affection suit. Sewell was a friend of Buster's sister Louise and was somewhat notorious for her easy-going morality, not least for having been involved in a wife-swapping divorce suit along with her husband Burton. Scriven later tried unsuccessfully to sue Paramount for $5 million for libel over *The Buster Keaton Story*.

Three on a Limb

Directed by: Charles Lamont
Produced by: E.H. Allen
Presented by: E.W. Hammons
Story by: Vernon Smith
Released: 3 January 1936
Length: 20 minutes (2 reels)

Cast:
Buster Keaton – Elmer Brown
Lona Andre – Molly
Harold Goodwin – Homer the cop
Grant Withers – Oscar
Barbara Bedford – Addie
John Ince – Molly's father
Fern Emmett – Molly's mother
Phyllis Crane – Molly's friend the car-hop

Photographed by: Gus Peterson
Sound by: Earl C. Sitar
Production company: Educational Films Corporation
Distributed by: Twentieth Century-Fox Film Corporation

> Stopping at a roadside burger joint, scoutmaster Elmer falls for waitress Molly. The trouble is, she has two other suitors – Homer the cop, favoured by her father, and Oscar the hood, her mother's preferred son-in-law. For his part, Oscar hasn't managed to shake off Addie, his previous girl. Put all seven in the family apartment, add a Justice of the Peace, and things get very lively indeed.

The supporting cast illustrate the unglamorous nature of Educational Films' 1930s output particularly well, many appearing in low budget exploitation films of the period. The following year, Fern Emmett would feature in the drug exposé *Assassin of Youth*, and Lona André would appear in both *Race Suicide*, a film about an abortion ring, and *Slaves in Bondage*, of which we need say no more.

The short was released a day after Buster's latest feature length film.

As was mentioned earlier, Buster had been hospitalised in October 1935 for his alcoholism (or "nervous exhaustion and influenza" as the press reported it in those very different times), and for a time was in a straitjacket in the psychiatric ward of the US Veterans General Hospital in West Los Angeles. Following the doctors' warnings, he managed to stay off alcohol for pretty much the next five years, and as a result appears more lively than in his previous two or three films.

On 29 January 1936, *Variety* announced Mrs. Mae Keaton's marriage to Sam Fuller, Hollywood publicist. "Bride's decree from Buster Keaton doesn't become final until October," the report added.

Grand Slam Opera

Directed by: Charles Lamont
Produced by: E.H. Allen
Presented by: E.W. Hammons
Story by: Buster Keaton, Charles Lamont
Released: 21 February 1936
Length: 20 minutes (2 reels, 1,860 feet)

Cast:
Buster Keaton – Elmer Butts
Diana Lewis – The girl downstairs
Harold Goodwin – Band leader
John Ince – Colonel Crow
Melrose Coakley – Member of Elmer's farewell party
Bud Jamison – Arizona sheriff, member of Elmer's farewell party
Lynton Brent – Sound engineer (uncredited)
Phyllis Crane – Girl with towels (uncredited)
Eddie Fetherston – Chauffeur (uncredited)

Photographed by: Gus Peterson
Sound by: Karl Zint
Production company: Educational Films Corporation
Distributed by: Twentieth Century-Fox Film Corporation

> Having been sung out of town from Gopher City, Arizona, for unstated misdeeds, Elmer heads for the big city intent on exhibiting his vaudeville skills on Colonel Crow's Amateur Night radio show. Fate relentlessly throws him in the company of a pancake flipping girl, who consistently refuses his offer of a little dinner and a show. Finally getting his spot on the radio show, Elmer elects to impress the listeners with his juggling.

This is easily the best of Buster's Educational Films shorts, which is certainly related to it being made just after he had stopped drinking as well as being the only one for which he receives a writing credit. As Eleanor Keaton confirms in *Buster Keaton Remembered*, it is also the only one of the Educational shorts that Buster actually liked.

Although Buster had been making talkies for over five years, the film neatly highlights the incongruity of a silent star in a talking picture performing a juggling routine on the radio. The minimal amount of dialogue – something Buster always advocated – also works well.

Buster was one of the few members of the cast not to have appeared on radio, Melrose Coakley and Bud Jamison in particular were well known on Pacific Coast radio.

Grand Slam Opera uniquely starts with a song from Buster, serenading the gunslingers who are running him out of town with "So Long, Elmer" to the tune of George M. Cohan's "So Long, Mary". The production company refused to pay for the rights to the tune, so Buster stumped up $300 of his own money to enable it to be included in the sequence. The film also includes far more of

Buster with
Harold Goodwin

Buster's dancing than we're used to, including a memorable pastiche of Fred Astaire's "No Strings" number from *Top Hat*, in which Astaire's energetic tap and sand dancing disturbs Ginger Rogers, trying to sleep in the room below.

Colonel Crow's Amateur Night is a parody of the "Major Bowes Amateur Hour", which ran on NBC and CBS radio from 1935 to 1945. A 20-year-old Frank Sinatra and 11-year-old Maria Callas had appeared on early editions of the show.

The sequence where Buster and Harold Goodwin whack each other with a baton and a broom in time to "The Anvil Chorus" harks back to The Three Keatons routines, and is reminiscent of the Marx Brothers' routines from *The Cocoanuts* and *Animal Crackers*.

Blue Blazes

Directed by: Raymond Kane, Buster Keaton (uncredited)
Produced by: Al Christie
Presented by: E.W. Hammons
Story by: David Freedman
Released: 21 August 1936
Length: 19 minutes (2 reels)

Cast:
Buster Keaton – Elmer
Arthur L. Jarrett – Fire chief
Rose Kessner – The chief's wife
Patty Wilson – The chief's brunette daughter
Marlyn Stuart – The chief's blonde daughter

Photographed by: George Webber
Production company: Educational Films Corporation
Distributed by: Twentieth Century-Fox Film Corporation

The patience of the chief of the city fire station is wearing thin and he relegates incompetent Elmer to an out-of-town station where they've had no fire for years. On his first day an alarm sounds, but on the way to the blaze Elmer is flung from the back of the engine as it turns a corner. Trying to find his way back to the station he calls at a house that happens to be that of the city fire chief. The enraged chief sends Elmer on his way, and vents his anger on his daughters by confining them to their room for the evening. The daughters, keen to be out with their firemen boyfriends, decide they can get out by starting a fire in a waste paper bin. Which naturally soon gets out of control. The fire crew are still out on a call – but maybe Elmer can finally prove himself, despite turning up on a bike, dragging a ladder, buckets and hose in his wake.

In April 1936, it was reported that Buster had signed with producer I.E. Chadwick for two feature-length comedies. In July 1936, it was further reported that Chadwick had acquired the rights to the story "Off Color" as a vehicle for Buster. Nothing seems to have come of the project.

Blue Blazes was the first for a new six-picture contract that Buster had signed in March with Educational Pictures at the Astoria studios in New York, initially under the control of Al Christie. The working title was *The Fourth Alarm*. It had been six months since Buster's previous release.

Buster's ongoing sobriety may have helped his performances to be appreciated by the critics – *Variety* noted that he "manipulates his comedy lines better than in his recent efforts".

Both of the actresses playing the chief's daughters had limited movie careers. Patty Wilson appeared in just one other film, and Scottish actress Marlyn Stuart was in a total of five films, three of which were with Buster. Fire chief Arthur Jarrett would co-write *Mixed Magic*, released in November.

Educational

BLUE BLAZES: Buster Keaton—Buster is always liked here, and this gave satisfaction, although it is not his best. Running time, 18 minutes.—A. N. Miles, Eminence Theatre, Eminence, Ky. Small town patronage.

CHEMIST, THE: Two-Reel Comedies — Swell comedy. Had all howling and pleased all.—Running time, 19 minutes.—R. J. Schmitt, Star Theatre, Geneva, Ind. General patronage.

The Chemist

Directed by: Al Christie
Produced by: Al Christie
Presented by: E.W. Hammons
Story by: David Freedman
Released: 9 October 1936
Length: 19 minutes (2 reels)

Cast:
Buster Keaton – Elmer "Happy" Triple
Marlyn Stuart – The girl
Earl Gilbert – The Professor
Don McBride – Gangster
Herman Lieb – Gangster
Eddie Hall – Gangster (uncredited)

Photographed by: George Webber
Production company: Educational Films Corporation
Distributed by: Twentieth Century-Fox Film Corporation

In the laboratory of Duncemore College, Elmer's string of inventions include a love potion, an enlarging agent – and a noiseless explosive. News of this reaches a team of gangsters who decide that they can get their hands on the new explosive, and so carry out noiseless safe-cracking, by enrolling at the college. So, while waiting to be escorted to a demonstration of his invention, Elmer is met by the slightly suspicious looking trio of Professor "Killer" Gerkin, Professor "Leftie" Doyle and Professor "Mugsy" Schultz, who instead escort him and his noiseless explosive to the Easy Payment Loan Company. A mix up in the powders thwarts the robbery, but the love potion ensures a happy ending.

During the filming of *The Chemist* in July, Natalie instigated a court action seeking alimony payments that she alleged he had missed. The case was heard at the end of the year – see p. 151.

Eddie Hall, playing "Mugsy" Schultz, is the only one of the gangsters not to receive a film credit.

Apart from its fleeting appearance as part of a gag in *Steamboat Bill, Jr.*, Buster's trademark porkpie hat re-emerges for the first time since *Go West* in 1925.

In 1936, a survey of the Motion Picture Producers and Distributors Association was held to discover how many actors were under contract to the studios for six months or more. Metro (MGM) led the field with 58 men and 48 women under contract. Bottom of the list was Educational with just one contract player – Buster Keaton.

Mixed Magic

Directed by: Raymond Kane, Buster Keaton (uncredited)
Produced by: General Service Studios
Presented by: E.W. Hammons
Story by: Arthur Jarrett, Marcy Klauber
Released: 20 November 1936
Length: 16 minutes (2 reels)

Cast:
Buster Keaton – Elmer "Happy" Butterworth
Eddie Lambert – The Great Professor Spumoni
Marlyn Stuart – Mary
Eddie Hall – Hector
Jimmie Fox
Walter Fenner – Circus manager
Pass Le Noir – Audience member
Harry Myers (uncredited)

Photographed by: George Webber
Production company: Educational Films Corporation
Distributed by: Twentieth Century-Fox Film Corporation

> The Great Spumoni sacks his sidekick and hires Buster, who has fallen for Spumoni's glamorous assistant, Mary. The disgruntled ex-sidekick then sets out to sabotage the Great Spumoni's act, although Buster manages to do this pretty well all by himself.

This was the last of three shorts that were filmed in New York.

Buster's line when he runs out of ducks to send up through the trap door, "that's all there is, there isn't any more", although now long forgotten, was famous at the time for being said by Ethel Barrymore to enthusiastic audiences clamouring for another curtain call.

The improbably named Pass Le Noir, who plays an audience member, was primarily a stage actress, and seems to have just one other on-screen credit, with Don Ameche in *Happy Land* in 1943.

Jail Bait

Directed by: Charles Lamont
Produced by: E.H. Allen (uncredited)
Presented by: E.W. Hammons
Story by: Paul Gerard Smith
Released: 8 January 1937
Length: 19 minutes (2 reels)

Cast:
Buster Keaton – The office boy
Harold Goodwin – The reporter
Matthew Betz – "Sawed-off" Madison
Bud Jamison – The detective
Betty Andre – The girl
Stanley Blystone – Arresting officer (uncredited)
Bobby Burns – Warden (uncredited)
Allan Cavan – Desk Sergeant (uncredited)
Harry Tenbrook – Prison guard (uncredited)

Photographed by: Dwight Warren
Sound by: William R. Fox
Production company: Educational Films Corporation
Distributed by: Twentieth Century-Fox Film Corporation

Office boy Buster is smitten with a girl at the newspaper office but can't afford a ring with which to woo her. Meanwhile police are investigating a murder, which his roommate, a reporter on the paper, is convinced has been committed by "Sawed-off" Madison. He needs Buster to falsely confess to keep the police off the scent while he chases up a lead. Buster does so, is jailed and shuns any opportunity to escape – until his discovers the reporter has been killed in a plane crash. Fortunately a jail break has been organised and he escapes with the gang responsible for it. Less fortunately, the jail break was organised by "Sawed-off" Madison who, when he finds out what Buster knows, determines to put him out of the picture. If only he could somehow bring Madison to justice, Buster would clear his name, scoop the reward and finally be able to afford the ring.

Betty André was the sister of Lona André, who had played the female lead in *One Run Elmer*, *The Timid Young Man* and *Three on a Limb*. Both tended to credit themselves without the accent on the final e.

Vaudeville writer Paul G. Smith had been taken on by Joseph Schenck to work with Buster as a staff writer in December 1925, but little seems to have come of it at that time. He was reported to have worked on *Battling Butler*, and then had a row with Buster during the filming of *The General*.

Just after filming *Jail Bait*, Buster's court case with Natalie over alimony and custody was heard at the New York Supreme Court. Natalie had sought Buster's entire earnings for 1936 for alimony arrears. Buster's response was that as he

Buster with Stanley Blystone

had turned over $500,000 in property and cash to Natalie when they divorced and was on a limited income, he had no money. He asked for his alimony to be reduced from $300 to $100 and separately sought custody of his two boys. In January the New York Supreme Court ruled that Natalie could have no more than 10% of Buster's earnings, and in August that his payments should be reduced to $100. Custody was denied.

Ditto

Directed by: Charles Lamont
Produced by: E.H. Allen (uncredited)
Presented by: E.W. Hammons
Story by: Paul Gerard Smith
Released: 12 February 1937
Length: 17 minutes (2 reels, 1,537 feet)

Cast:
Buster Keaton – The forgotten man
Gloria Brewster – Housewife
Barbara Brewster – Housewife's twin sister
Harold Goodwin – Hank
Lynton Brent – Bill
Al Thompson – Stable hand
Bob Ellsworth
Payne B. Johnson – Boy (uncredited)

Photographed by: Dwight Warren
Sound by: Earl C. Sitar
Production company: Educational Films Corporation
Distributed by: Twentieth Century-Fox Film Corporation

An ice-man's best friend is his horse, until he falls for a customer buying 20-cents worth for her icebox. With her twin sister living next door, and with both sisters being married anyway, opportunities are rife for confusion and disappointment. When the truth is revealed, Buster vows to escape to Canada for 15 years. When the time is up, his eye is caught by a woman returning from a fishing trip. He is invited over to her camp, and so shaves off 15 years of beard growth and heads over, flowers in hand. On seeing she is one of five identical quintuplets, he turns on his heels …

Buster's penultimate Educational Films picture was, as *Film Daily* informs us, the last film to be completed by any studio in 1936. It was the second of three once again produced by E.H. Allen and distributed by Twentieth Century-Fox.

Film Daily also reported on 21 January 1937 that Buster was scheduled to appear in an Oliver Hardy road show film – without Stan Laurel – to be directed by Norman McLeod and produced by Hal Roach. This became *Pick a Star*, and although Hal Roach did produce it, it was directed by Edward Sedgwick. In the end Buster didn't appear in the film, but Stan Laurel did. There was much talk around this time of there being something rotten in the state of Laurel and Hardy, and that the duo were on the verge of splitting. This didn't happen of course, but the *Pick a Star* production shenanigans were almost certainly a symptom or a result of this.

Love Nest on Wheels

Louise, Harry, Myra, Al St. John and Buster

Directed by: Charles Lamont
Produced by: E.H. Allen (uncredited)
Presented by: E.W. Hammons
Adapted by: Paul Gerard Smith
From the story by: William Hazlett Upson
Released: 26 March 1937
Length: 18 minutes (2 reels, 1,604 feet)

Cast:
Buster Keaton – Elmer
Myra Keaton – Elmer's Ma
Al St. John – Uncle Jed

Lynton Brent – The bridegroom
Diana Lewis – The bride
Bud Jamison – Potts, the mortgage holder
Louise Keaton – Elmer's sis
Harry Keaton – Elmer's brother
Payne B. Johnson – Boy (uncredited)

Photographed by: Dwight Warren
Sound by: Earl C. Sitar
Production company: Educational Films Corporation
Distributed by: Twentieth Century-Fox Film Corporation

> Another slow day at the Van Buren Hotel … until newlyweds arrive for the night, but only because it's the only hotel for 50 miles around. Dissatisfied with the room, they are persuaded by Elmer to buy a caravan for $350, which a city feller had left behind when he was shot. This would give the honeymooners the freedom of the road, and the family the money to pay off the mortgage on the hotel and prevent foreclosure. The only problem is, Uncle Jed's cow is stuck in the caravan.

Buster's last independent Buster Keaton Productions film was *The Love Nest*, and his final film for Educational is *Love Nest on Wheels*. It is better than most, largely thanks to the friends and family that bolster the cast. Al St. John makes a welcome return for his last Buster Keaton film – their 15th partnership – although both Buster and St. John would appear in supporting roles in *Li'l Abner* three years later. Brother Harry gets his only on-screen credit in a Buster film (although he'd had bit parts in *Convict 13* and *The Cameraman*), alongside their sister Louise, naturally playing Elmer's brother and sister. And pipe-smoking Myra is staunchly comic as Ma.

Eleanor Keaton described Myra as "a very independent lady. Standing just four feet ten inches tall, she rolled her own cigarettes and drank straight bourbon."

The plot reworks a number of gags from *The Bell Boy*, including a horse-powered elevator, which refused to budge and traps a group of guests between floors, and a fly-line transferring hot towels between the kitchen and the barber shop causing predictable mayhem.

Bridegroom Lynton Brent would also appear with Buster in five of his shorts for Columbia. In addition to acting he was an architect and a novelist. His works of gay pulp fiction include *Lesbian Gang* and *Sir Gay*, the story of the son of a deposed monarch who comes to Hollywood to discover a whole new world.

Having fulfilled his contract with Educational films, Buster decided not to renew. In July 1937 he signed up with MGM once more in the role of short subject director. Three one-reel shorts directed by Buster were released in 1938 – *Life in Sometown, USA*, *Hollywood Handicap* and *Streamlined Swing*. In October 1937 there were reports of Metro teaming up Buster with Buddy Ebsen and Ted Healy for a Marx Brothers-style ensemble, the brothers having recently signed with RKO. Eddie Sedgwick was lined up for their first production, but of course nothing came of it. Ted Healey died in December 1937.

THE COLUMBIA SHORTS

Directed by: Del Lord
Produced by: Jules White
Presented by: Columbia Pictures
Original screenplay by: Clyde Bruckman, Buster Keaton (uncredited)
Released: 16 June 1939
Length: 19 minutes (2 reels)

Cast:
Buster Keaton – Sir
Lorna Gray – Conchita
Gino Corrado – Martino
Richard Fiske – Ferdinand the bullfighter
Bobby Barber – Musician (uncredited)
James Craig – Pedro (uncredited)
Charles Dorety – Musician (uncredited)
Ned Glass – Deck hand (uncredited)
Bud Jamison – Neighbour taking siesta (uncredited)
Eddie Laughton – Deck hand (uncredited)
Forbes Murray – Butler (uncredited)
Robert Sterling – Cigarette customer at adjacent table (uncredited)

Photography by: Henry Freulich
Film editor: Charles Nelson
Sound by: Edward Bernds (uncredited)
Production company: Columbia Pictures
Distributed by: Columbia Pictures

Buster moors his yacht in Mexico and, suitably attired, checks out the local town. Here Conchita has accepted an engagement ring from Martino, with the caveat that he will kill any man who tries to woo her. Unfortunately she is in love with Ferdinand, who realises that if Martino sees her with another man and kills him, he will go to jail and they can be married. Buster is naturally singled out as that other man. Using the tried and tested formula of hitting her over the head with a guitar, Buster has Conchita fall in love with him, necessitating him fighting a duel with both Martino and Ferdinand.

Buster, "trying a comeback as a comic" as *Variety* sensitively put it, signed with Columbia in March 1939, initially to make two short films, with options for additional two-reelers. He would earn just $2,500 per short – half his Educational

Pictures salary. The films were delivered free to theatres playing Columbia features and so were the studio's lowest priority. Buster referred to the films as "cheaters" as they were churned out as cheaply and as quickly as possible.

Buster was reunited with writer Clyde Bruckman, collaborator on many of his feature length films, for this and seven other Columbia shorts.

The film uses material from *The Invader*, including the rendition of "In a Little Spanish Town" (music by Mabel Wayne, lyrics by Sam Lewis and Joe Young), which works much better in this condensed format, being rather less laboured. Being the first of the series, this film's production values, with location shooting and a substantial set, are noticeably higher than would be the case as time went on. As such, it was exceptionally well received, *Film Daily* pointing out that "when a comedy shown cold in a projection room can make trade press critics howl in their seats" it has to be a winner. Certainly Buster considered this the best of his Columbia series.

The harbour scenes were shot at Newport Beach, where Buster had shot scenes for *The Boat* and *College*.

Once again Buster offers to treat the leading lady to a little dinner and a show.

In June 1939, Twentieth Century-Fox announced a Coming Attraction – *Falling Stars*, starring Alice Faye, Don Ameche and Buster Keaton. This was the working title for *Hollywood Cavalcade*, which Buster shot having completed *Pest from the West*.

The titles of the Columbia shorts started to feature an image of Buster.

Mooching Through Georgia

Directed by: Jules White
Produced by: Jules White
Presented by: Columbia Pictures
Original screenplay by: Clyde Bruckman, Buster Keaton (uncredited)
Released: 11 August 1939
Length: 19 minutes (2 reels)

Cast:
Buster Keaton – Homer Cobb
Monte Collins – Cyrus Cobb, Homer's brother
Jill Martin – Lula Belle
Bud Jamison – Titus Cobb aka Pa
Lynton Brent – Union Colonel (uncredited)
Heinie Conklin – Union soldier (uncredited)
Jack Cooper – Confederate soldier (uncredited)
Nick Copeland – Union soldier (uncredited)
Lew Davis – Union soldier (uncredited)
Ned Glass – Union Sgt. veteran Zeb Montagu (uncredited)
Jack Hill – Union officer (uncredited)
Johnny Kascier – Union officer (uncredited)
Stanley Mack – Confederate Major (uncredited)
Joe Murphy – Tall Union soldier (uncredited)
Cy Schindell – Union soldier (uncredited)

Photography by: John Stumar
Film editor: Arthur Seid
Music by: William Grant Still (uncredited)
Production company: Columbia Pictures
Distributed by: Columbia Pictures

> Civil war veterans are reminiscing in a rest home. Homer relates the story of how he inadvertently enlisted on the Confederate rather than the Union side. In attempting to swap his uniform he finds himself taken prisoner by his brother Cyrus, and then, when the Confederate soldiers arrive in town, vice versa. Bursting into a Union strategy meeting, Homer steals a map and embarks on a convoluted quest to get it to the Confederate camp.

Jill Martin has gone under a number of guises in a varied life. She was born Evelyn Merchant in 1913, but after her parents died she was fostered by Mr. and

Mrs. Cowan, and became Evelyn Cowan. She appeared in a handful of films in the late 1930s as Harlene Wood or – yes, hooray for her – Harley Wood. Her last three credited performances were as Jill Martin, however. In 1940 she married Felix Jackson, and after their divorce she then married Seymour (Sy) Miller. As Jill Jackson-Miller, she co-wrote the popular song "Let There Be Peace on Earth" with her husband.

Monte Collins, who was also in *Sidewalks of New York*, *General Nuisance* and *She's Oil Mine* (billed by Columbia as Monty Collins) was the son of Monte Collins, who appeared in *The Playhouse*, *My Wife's Relations* and *Our Hospitality*.

Once again, Buster uses a stand-in for a close up of his right hand gathering ants in a mug, as he did for a similar close up in *Three Ages*, as he was missing the tip of his right forefinger.

Johnny Kascier acts a stunt double for Buster in the film, as he does for a scene in *General Nuisance*. The couple of stunts he is used for are relatively straightforward – jumping on a horse and riding a penny farthing bicycle – whereas elsewhere Buster executes arguably more difficult stunts, and rather better.

In August 1939, Twentieth Century-Fox released *Quick Millions*, directed by Malcolm St. Clair. This was the second of two Fox films based on original stories by Buster and Joseph Hoffman – *The Jones Family in Hollywood*, also directed by St. Clair, was released two months earlier.

On 29 August, Columbia announced it had renewed Buster's writer-actor contract for a further two shorts under Jules White, to be written by Clyde Bruckman.

Nothing But Pleasure

Directed by: Jules White
Produced by: Jules White
Presented by: Columbia Pictures
Story and screenplay by: Clyde Bruckman
Released: 19 January 1940
Length: 17 minutes (2 reels)

Cast:
Buster Keaton – Clarence Plunkett
Dorothy Appleby – Mrs. Plunkett
Beatrice Blinn – Intoxicated woman
Bobby Barber – Snacking bus rider (uncredited)
Lynton Brent – Sheriff at Cozy Auto Court (uncredited)
Vernon Dent – Bus rider with child (uncredited)

Charles Dorety – Roadside workman (uncredited)
Richard Fiske – Man with damaged car in Detroit (uncredited)
Bud Jamison – Cop in Detroit (uncredited)
Johnny Kascier – Man on ladder (uncredited)
Eddie Laughton – Gangster at Cozy Auto Court (uncredited)
John Rand – Farmer (uncredited)
Jack Randall (uncredited)
Robert Sterling – Gangster at Cozy Auto Court (uncredited)
Victor Travis – Deputy (uncredited)
John Tyrrell – Car salesman in Detroit (uncredited)
Dorothy Vernon – Snoring bus rider (uncredited)

Director of photography: Henry Freulich
Film editor: Arthur Seid
Music by: William Grant Still (uncredited)
Production company: Columbia Pictures
Distributed by: Columbia Pictures

Clarence Plunkett sells his car in order to go to Detroit to buy a new one direct from the factory and drive back to California, saving money in the process. His wife reluctantly goes along with him. On the way home they stop off at a bungalow park and find themselves in the middle of a shoot-out between the police and a band of bank robbers. The robbers make off in Clarence's new car, giving him an incentive in helping to bring them to justice.

"Nothing But Pleasure"
(*Columbia*)

Buster Keaton, in his artless way, becomes involved in a series of misadventures which wind up in some hilarious scenes. He sells his old car and travels with his wife, Dorothy Appleby, to Detroit to purchase a new one. He neglects to buy insurance and his car is wrecked by bandits. Highlighting the comedy is a scene where Keaton attempts to put an inebriated lady to bed. Running time, 17 mins.

The film includes a version of Buster's beloved putting-a-drunk-woman-to-bed routine, originally seen in *Spite Marriage*. It is obviously still a winner as *Motion Picture Daily* singles it out in its review – "Highlighting the comedy is a scene where Keaton attempts to put an inebriated lady to bed." Buster would develop this into a full 12-minute routine (to the tune of "Two Sleepy People") which, for example, he would use to great effect on tour in Toronto, Paris and Las Vegas in late 1952.

Buster himself would often go to Detroit to buy a new car direct from the factory and drive it home.

The car parking sequence is one Clyde Bruckman borrowed from his 1935 film with W.C. Fields, *Man on the Flying Trapeze*.

Pardon My Berth Marks

Directed by: Jules White
Produced by: Jules White
Presented by: Columbia Pictures
Story and screenplay by: Clyde Bruckman
Released: 22 March 1940
Length: 18 minutes (2 reels)

Cast:
Buster Keaton – Elmer, newspaper copyboy
Dorothy Appleby – Mary Christman
Richard Fiske – Ted Christman, racketeer
Vernon Dent – Mr. Boggle, newspaper editor
Symona Boniface – Train passenger (uncredited)
Lynton Brent – Train passenger (uncredited)
Stanley Brown – Newlywed (uncredited)
Ned Glass – Wedding guest in train station (uncredited)
Bud Jamison – Train conductor (uncredited)
Isabel La Mal – Mary's aunt (uncredited)
Eddie Laughton – Train passenger (uncredited)
Jack "Tiny" Lipson – Angry man in Pullman berth (uncredited)
Eva McKenzie – Ma (uncredited)
Cy Schindell – Al Spumoni, mobster (uncredited)
Fred "Snowflake" Toones – Train porter (uncredited)
Victor Travis – Train passenger (uncredited)
John Tyrrell – Train passenger (uncredited)
Dorothy Vernon – Train passenger (uncredited)

Director of photography: Benjamin Kline
Film editor: Mel Thorson
Production company: Columbia Pictures
Distributed by: Columbia Pictures

> Mary Christman ("and a Happy New Year!") has discovered her husband is a racketeer and not the society manager he told her he was, and so she is taking the train to Reno for a divorce. News reaches the local newspaper and, as all reporters are out on stories, the editor has no choice but to send office boy Elmer – with his parrot Clarice – to pursue the lead. They are joined en route by Mary's angry husband Ted, who assumes Elmer's relationship with Mary is less than honourable. Despite being let down by Clarice, Elmer gets a scoop that earns him a job as a reporter.

Eva McKenzie, playing Buster's mother, was married to Robert McKenzie, who appeared with Buster in *Hayseed Romance*.

The script owes more than a little to Laurel and Hardy's 1929 short *Berth Marks*.

In March 1940, Buster signed for a further two shorts, and shooting also began on *The Villain Still Pursued Her*, the first of three RKO features that he would make over the following three or four years. It would be directed by Buster's old friend Eddie Cline, and interestingly the announcement of the start of production in *Film Daily* gave Buster top billing.

The Taming of the Snood

Directed by: Jules White
Produced by: Jules White
Presented by: Columbia Pictures
Story and screenplay by: Ewart Adamson, Clyde Bruckman
Released: 28 June 1940
Length: 16 minutes (2 reels)

Cast:
Buster Keaton – Buster
Elsie Ames – Odette, the maid
Dorothy Appleby – Miss Wilson
Bruce Bennett – Detective (uncredited)
Stanley Brown – Photographer (uncredited)
Vernon Dent – Man on street (uncredited)
Richard Fiske – Detective (uncredited)

Director of photography: Henry Freulich
Film editor: Mel Thorson

Music by: William Grant Still (uncredited)
Production company: Columbia Pictures
Distributed by: Columbia Pictures

> A jewel thief slips into Keaton's Snappy Hats to evade the detectives on her trail. She hides a stolen ring in milliner Buster's porkpie hat, buys it from him and asks for it to be delivered to her apartment. After much improvised slapstick between Buster and the drunken maid, the jewel (bear with me on this) ends up strapped to a parrot. When the parrot escapes, Buster is persuaded to climb after it onto the apartment's ledge. In spite of help from the maid, he somehow fails to plummet to his death and the detectives get their gal.

The film uses the same aerial shots of the city street as *So You Won't Squawk*.

This is the first of five films pairing Buster with Elsie Ames. It's possible that Columbia had a double act in mind, along the lines of Keaton–Durante, although as with that coupling, Ames' larger than life personality is rather to Buster's detriment.

The lengthy sequence involving the table is almost certainly based on The 'Three Keatons' vaudeville act (the act, with Buster's brother Jingles on board, was on occasion billed along the lines of "The man with the table, wife and two kids").

Richard Fiske plays one of the detectives in his fourth and final short with Buster. He was drafted into the US Army a couple of years later and was killed in action in Normandy in 1944.

The Spook Speaks

Directed by: Jules White
Produced by: Jules White
Presented by: Columbia Pictures
Story and screenplay by: Ewart Adamson, Clyde Bruckman
Released: 20 September 1940
Length: 18 minutes (2 reels)

Cast:
Buster Keaton – Buster
Elsie Ames – Elsie
Don Beddoe – Newlywed husband
Dorothy Appleby – Newlywed wife
Bruce Bennett – Mordini's former assistant (uncredited)
Lynton Brent – Mordini, magician and spiritualist (uncredited)
John Tyrrell – Mordini's assistant (uncredited)
Evelyn Young – Former assistant's girlfriend (uncredited)

Director of photography: Henry Freulich
Film editor: Mel Thorson
Music by: Leigh Harline, Howard Jackson, Ben Oakland, William Grant Still
  (uncredited)
Production company: Columbia Pictures
Distributed by: Columbia Pictures

> Buster and Elsie are caretakers sent to look after the house of Professor Mordini, magician and spiritualist, who is wary of a former assistant out to steal his tricks. Left alone in the house for the night, they are soon joined by a newlywed couple, and unknowingly by the former assistant and his girlfriend. With the new bride also being a spiritualist and the former assistant using the house's in-built tricks to scare Buster and Elsie, the stage is set for a series of low-par antics. Throw in a roller-skating penguin, a flying banjo, a power cut, and we almost have a plot.

Probably the weakest of the Columbia shorts, despite being co-written by Clyde Bruckman, who was in poor health at the time. Nevertheless reviews were generally positive as usual, for instance *Film Daily* reckoned the gag with the musical jug "should get real belly laughs", and the film was also a hit with the public, an exhibitor reported in the *Motion Picture Herald*, "Went over big with our audiences. This old timer still means something at the box office and deserves splendid mention in your newspaper ads."

Much of the central sequence is borrowed from Harold Lloyd's first talkie, *Welcome Danger*, which was also directed by Clyde Bruckman.

On 20 September 1940, the day of release of *The Spook Speaks*, Buster appeared in the chorus of Charlot's Revue, which was put on at El Capitan Theatre in Hollywood to raise money for British War Charities. With him in the male chorus were the likes of Henry Fonda and Ronald Colman. Rita Hayworth and Freddie Bartholomew were among the luminaries who also took part.

His Ex Marks the Spot

Directed by: Jules White
Produced by: Jules White
Presented by: Columbia Pictures
Story and screenplay by: Felix Adler
Released: 13 December 1940
Length: 18 minutes (2 reels)

Cast:
Buster Keaton – Buster, the husband
Elsie Ames – His ex-wife
Matt McHugh – Radcliffe, the ex-wife's boyfriend
Dorothy Appleby – Buster's wife
Jack "Tiny" Lipson – Repossession man (uncredited)
John Tyrrell – Justice of the Peace (uncredited)

Director of photography: Benjamin Kline
Film editor: Mel Thorson
Production company: Columbia Pictures
Distributed by: Columbia Pictures

Buster and his current wife are struggling to make ends meet. So, to avoid having to pay his ex-wife $30 alimony, he hits on the bright idea of inviting her – and her "friend" Radcliffe, who elevates irritating to an art form – to move in with them. A shotgun wedding resolves the ensuing domestic uproar.

The scene is which Buster struggles to carve the chicken is lifted from *The Sidewalks of New York*, also (co-)directed by Jules White.

Having just completed filming of *L'il Abner* for RKO and signed a new deal with Columbia for three more two-reelers, Buster began shooting *His Ex Marks the Spot* on 26 September.

The film was re-released in June 1950 as a so-called Columbia Comedy Favorite.

Writer Felix Adler was originally a vaudeville actor and circus clown.

So You Won't Squawk

Directed by: Del Lord
Produced by: Del Lord, Hugh McCollum
Presented by: Columbia Pictures
Story and screenplay by: Elwood Ullman
Released: 21 February 1941
Length: 16 minutes (2 reels)

Cast:
Buster Keaton – Eddie
Matt McHugh – Louie the Wolf's henchman
Eddie Fetherston – Louie the Wolf's henchman
Lane Chandler – 2nd cop (uncredited)
Edmund Cobb – 1st cop (uncredited)
Marjorie Deanne – Miss Flo (uncredited)
Vernon Dent – Savoy bartender (uncredited)
Bud Jamison – Tom (uncredited)
Hank Mann – Island Inn workman (uncredited)
Duke York – 1st Motorcycle Cop (uncredited)

Director of photography: Benjamin Kline
Film editor: Arthur Seid
Production company: Columbia Pictures
Distributed by: Columbia Pictures

Handyman Eddie is working on Louie the Wolf's club, when he inadvertently thwarts a little trouble from rival gangster Slugger McGraw's henchmen. As a result, the henchmen assume Eddie is Louie the Wolf, and Louie is happy to go along with this and sit back while his rivals go to great lengths to wipe Eddie out. With each assassination attempt, Eddie contrives to escape death. Finally wise to the situation, Eddie rounds up as many cops as possible with a series of traffic violations to confront Louie the Wolf.

On 30 April 1941, *Variety* reported that Buster ("once a star in his own right") had signed up for a featured role in Republic studio's *Puddin' Head*, starring Judy Canova, which had started shooting two days earlier. Filming had been delayed because of casting disputes between the star and Republic's studio head. However, a fortnight later he had pulled out of the project "because of illness". This was likely alcohol-related because, although Buster's drinking was nowhere near as serious as in the early 1930s, he still had his moments.

The script includes a sequence where Buster crashes into a wagon full of chickens – hence the title. Unfortunately the scene is not in the film, making the title more incongruous than usual.

This was probably a stock script, not written for Buster. It is one of only two Columbia shorts not written by Clyde Bruckman, and is the only one of all Buster's films to be written by Elwood Ullman. It is also the only time Buster is given the workaday name of Eddie.

General Nuisance

Directed by: Jules White
Produced by: Jules White
Presented by: Columbia Pictures
Story and screenplay by: Clyde Bruckman, Felix Adler
Released: 18 September 1941
Length: 18 minutes (2 reels)

Cast:
Buster Keaton – Peter Hedley Lamar Jr.
Elsie Ames – Elsie, army nurse
Dorothy Appleby – Dorothy, army nurse
Monte Collins – Sgt. Michael Collins
Nick Arno – Recruiting doctor (uncredited)
Bobby Barber – Orderly (uncredited)
Lynton Brent – Captain (uncredited)
Bud Jamison – General (uncredited)
Johnny Kascier – 2nd orderly, stuntman (uncredited)
Cy Schindell – Crazy patient with cleaver (uncredited)
Harry Semels – Latin American delegate (uncredited)
John Tyrrell – Delegate's aide (uncredited)

Director of photography: Benjamin Kline
Film editor: Jerome Thoms
Production company: Columbia Pictures
Distributed by: Columbia Pictures

Millionaire Peter Hedley Lamar Jr. happens to meet army nurse Dorothy and it's love at first sight. But Dorothy only falls for men in uniform, so naturally Lamar enlists. A song and dance number with her friend Elsie later and he's still no nearer winning over Dorothy, so he sets out to injure himself to get under her tender care. Cupid finally triumphs thanks to a case of concussion resulting from the actions of an axe-wielding patient.

Nick Arno, who plays the recruiting doctor, was married to Elsie Ames.

The dance routine was choreographed by Buster and Elsie Ames in around two hours, according to director Jules White.

In getting Buster to hospital, Elsie Ames uses a wheelbarrow in a variation of Buster's putting-a-drunk-woman-to-bed routine.

The film uses material seen in *Doughboys* – not least the fact that, for the last time, Buster tries to entice his leading lady to a little dinner and a show.

It had been seven months since Buster's last release. In the summer of 1941, he toured various summer theatres – so-called "straw-hat" seasons – in the play *North* and the 1920s murder mystery *The Gorilla*. The first performance of the final leg in Westboro, Massachusetts, at the beginning of September had to be cancelled as he had gone "missing" en route from Toledo, Ohio. He was finally located at the luxury Essex House hotel in New York, and put on a train for Westboro. There was no mention of the reasons for this in the press, *Variety* reporting that "Management announced Keaton was 'grounded' while flying from Toledo, O."

Buster with Dorothy Ames

She's Oil Mine

Directed by: Jules White
Produced by: Jules White
Presented by: Columbia Pictures
Story and screenplay by: Felix Adler, Clyde Bruckman (uncredited)
Released: 20 November 1941
Length: 18 minutes (2 reels)

Cast:
Buster Keaton – Buster Waters, plumber
Elsie Ames – Elsie
Monte Collins – Monty Piper, plumber
Eddie Laughton – Clemente, Elsie's suitor
Dorothy Appleby – Maid (uncredited)
Jacqueline Dalya – Yvette (uncredited)
Bud Jamison – Second (uncredited)
Harry Semels – Referee (uncredited)
Jules White – Voice of radio announcer (uncredited)

Director of photography: Benjamin Kline
Film editor: Jerome Thoms
Production company: Columbia Pictures
Distributed by: Columbia Pictures

Oil heiress Elsie has come to realise that her lover Clemente is only good for one thing, and that's kissing. So, more often than not she is trying to escape his attention. It comes to pass that on one such occasion she ducks into Waters and Piper, plumbers, and hides inside a boiler. When the coast is clear she takes the opportunity to ask them to fix her shower. After a spot of confusion in Elsie's bathroom, Clemente turns up and finds Buster with Elsie but without his shirt – and so slaps his face, offers his card and challenges him to a duel. The following morning, with duellers, seconders and referee assembled, Buster shows his ignorance of the niceties of fighting duels by slapping everyone's face and accepting their card ("business is picking up!"). Happily he escapes a sticky end thanks to a passing hunter firing off a shotgun.

Shortly before filming *She's Oil Mine*, Buster had completed his part in the third chapter of the all-star Anglo-American charity film *Forever and a Day*, which would be released in 1943.

She's Oil Mine owes a heavy debt to *The Passionate Plumber*, including the duelling scene. It is a virtual shot-for-shot remake of the first 15 minutes of the earlier film with Monte Collins standing in for Jimmy Durante. This scene was a favourite with Buster, and he often performed it on his later tours. Buster probably liked the scene so much as he is largely silent, with the dialogue happening all around him.

This last Columbia short was one of the most popular, and the company offered to renew Buster's contract. But he had clearly had enough of the two-reel comedies and so turned Columbia down, preferring to go back to MGM as a gag writer. One benefit of having done the Columbia shorts was the fact that because they accompanied Columbia features, they reached a wider audience than the Educational Pictures two-reelers, leading to more offers of work than he had received when he was with Educational.

It was also Buster's last film with his long-time collaborator Clyde Bruckman, although Bruckman was a producer for *The Buster Keaton Show* in 1951. He had also directed Harold Lloyd and The Three Stooges – as well as W.C. Fields' glorious short *The Fatal Glass of Beer* in 1933 (as good an excuse as any to include a still from the film). But by the 1950s work had all but dried up for Bruckman, and he was beset by legal and alcohol problems. He borrowed a pistol from Buster, saying he wanted to go hunting, and on 4 January 1955, drove to a local restaurant, disappeared into the restroom and shot himself in the head. It was a terrible echo of his own father's suicide in similar circumstances in 1912.

W.C. Fields serenades Richard Cramer in *The Fatal Glass of Beer*

THE INDEPENDENT YEARS

El Moderno Barba Azul

Aka *The Modern Bluebeard*
Aka *Boom in the Moon* (US)

Directed by: Jaime Salvador
Produced by: Alejandro Salkind
Presented by: Alejandro Salkind
Screenplay by: Victor Trivas, Jaime Salvador
Based on original idea by: Victor Trivas
Released: 1946
Length: 68 minutes (US)

Cast:
Buster Keaton
Ángel Garasa
Virginia Serret
Fernando Soto
Luis G. Barreiro
Jorge Mondragón
Óscar Pulido
José Elías Moreno
Pitouto
Francisco D. Valero
Ramon G. Larrea
Francisco Martinez
Roberto Carduño
Angel Buenafuente
Guillermo Bravo Sosa
Fernando Flaguer
Pedro Elviro (uncredited)
Ignacio Peón (uncredited)
Enriqueta Reza (uncredited)
José Torvay (uncredited)

Director of photography: Agustin Jiminez
  (uncredited)
Camera operator: Ernesto U. Vazquez
  (uncredited)
Edited by: Rafael Ceballos (uncredited)
Sound by: B.J. Kroger, Eduardo Fernandez
Music by: Georges Tzipine, Leo Cardona
  (uncredited)
Production company: Alsa Film

Keaton Mexico Venture

MEXICO CITY, July 23.—Buster Keaton is here to work in his first Mexican picture, "The Modern Bluebeard," which Alejandro Silkind is to produce early in August. Keaton brought his wife along.

> World War II is over, but Buster, adrift in a life raft, is blissfully unaware of the fact. Reaching land in what he thinks is Japan but is actually Mexico, he hands himself in. An administrative mix-up results in his captors thinking he is a modern Bluebeard who is on the run having killed six of his wives. Before he can be executed however, a nearby scientist kidnaps him and his cellmate to pilot his atomic rocket to the moon – his logic being they would prefer a trip into space to the electric chair. Confusion at the rocket's launch sees the scientist's niece join the former cellmates on their lunar adventure. But when they finally land on the moon, things seem strangely earth-like.

Buster's last starring role in a feature film is probably his worst yet, made on a minuscule budget with an alarmingly jaunty soundtrack. The linguistic confusion between Buster and his Spanish captors in the early part of the film is lost in the dubbed version, in which everyone speaks English. Even Buster is dubbed (well, mostly), which is doubly disconcerting.

Virtually all reference sources give the release date as 2 August 1946. However, although Buster signed up for the film in January 1946, press reports at the time, including in *Variety*, describe filming as having started on 29 August and continuing through September 1946.

Producer Alejandro Salkind is none other than Alexander Salkind, who was a Mexican citizen at the time, and who went on to be an executive producer on *Superman* in 1978, and a couple of its sequels. A second Mexican film with Salkind, *The Bandit*, was announced in May 1947, but failed to materialise.

The English-language version currently available is about fifteen minutes shorter than the original release, mainly missing scenes between Buster and Ángel Garasa in prison, eating together and playing cards.

Eleanor Keaton thought so little of the film that she wisely decided not to include stills from it in her lavish memoir *Buster Keaton Remembered*.

Un Duel à Mort

Directed by: Pierre Blondy
Produced by: René Bianco, Louis Lefait
Presented by: Les Films Cristal
Written by: Pierre Blondy, Buster Keaton
Released: 1948
Length: 24 minutes

Cast:
Buster Keaton – First fisherman
[Antonin] Berval – Second fisherman

Cinematography: Jacques Isnard
Cameraman: Jacques Natteau
Music by: Georges Van Parys
Production company: Films Azur

> Two fisherman become embroiled in a dispute when their lines become entangled and ownership of the single fish at the end of one line is at issue. The only way to resolve the situation is a duel …

The duelling scene from *The Passionate Plumber* and *She's Oil Mine* rears its head once more.

Buster made this three-reel short when he was in Paris at the Cirque Médrano. It failed to get a US release.

There is some confusion over the date of release. In Eleanor Keaton and Jeffrey Vance's *Buster Keaton Remembered* it is given as 7 September 1950, and online sources mainly plump for 1952. It was made during Buster's first trip to the Cirque Médrano however, which was in 1947.

Paradise for Buster

Directed by: Del Lord
Presented by: John Deere
Written by: J.P. Prindle, John Grey, Hal Goodwin
Released: 15 October 1952
Length: 39 minutes

Cast:
Buster Keaton – Buster
Harold Goodwin – Fisherman (uncredited)

Photography: J.J. LaFleur, Robert Sable
Sound recording: Everett Ryan
Film editor: William Minnerly
Musical score: Albert Glasser

Production company: Wilding Picture Productions, Inc.
Distributed by: John Deere and Co.

> Mr. Monroe of the Monroe Mining Company's patience finally runs out with his inept clerk Buster, but just as Buster hears he has inherited a farm from his uncle Burr McKeaton, and can therefore quit. The farm isn't up to much, and is actually about to be foreclosed, so it is no great loss when Buster accidentally burns it down. Having no luck harnessing the water stream or windmill, Buster decides there's not much point in carrying on, but just before ending it all by throwing himself in the farm's lake he notices that the lake is teeming with fish. Unsuccessful in his own attempts to catch any fish without the aid of a rifle, he hits upon the idea of opening Fisherman's Paradise: Buster Keaton, Prop.

This is probably the first of a number of so-called industrial films that Buster made. These were essentially glorified commercials made by private companies, and as such weren't widely distributed – if they were "released" at all – and so remain quite obscure, which also explains why the cast list here is so scant. Actors in the industrial films were rarely professionals and more often than not were employees of the advertised company. It's not known for certain how many of these industrial films that Buster made, but some of the key surviving ones are described here.

Although an industrial film, *Paradise for Buster* doesn't seek to promote any product or service and was most likely a gift to sales staff of the John Deere company, which still manufactures agricultural and construction machinery to this day.

Buster has two lines in the film – "Good morning", and "I quit". The film basically consists of gags from a handful of his earlier films – including the piggy bank scene from *The Cameraman*, the shattering glass in doors from *Pardon My Berth Marks*, the fishing attempts from *The Love Nest*, the suicide in *The Electric House*, and even back to the molasses from *The Butcher Boy*.

It was directed by Del Lord, his last film as director. A former Keystone Kop, Lord directed over 200 films, almost exclusively shorts, many of them with The Three Stooges, including *Pest from the West* and *So You Won't Squawk*.

Paradise for Buster was also Buster's eighth and final film with Harold Goodwin, who is credited as a co-writer. Goodwin had been working with Buster as writer and actor for his television shows in 1950–51.

The Devil to Pay

Directed by: Herb Skoble
Produced by: Education Research Films for the National Association of
  Wholesalers
Script: Cummins-Betts
Released: 1960
Length: 28 minutes

Cast:
Buster Keaton – Diablos
Ralph Dunn – The furnace man
Ruth Gillette – Minnie
Marion Morris – Esther
John Rodney – Druggist

Video: Del Ankers, Fritz Roland
Editing: Cummins-Betts
Animation and graphics: Pilgrim Film Services
Audio: Nelson Funk
Production company: Rodel Productions

A technical error causes a rocket launched from Earth to crash on the planet Hades, ruler Diablos. The crash destroys his bed of beloved dimorphotheca flowers. He travels to Earth to seek revenge. He happens to land near Minnie, a slightly unhinged civic activist campaigning to "eliminate the middleman". Diablos uses his telekinetic powers to force the population into writing to their Congressmen to do exactly that. The film veers into a wholesaler propaganda piece, complete with graphics and everything, demonstrating the catastrophic results of ditching the middleman.

Another industrial film, this one made for the National Association of Wholesalers. The promotional leaflet describes the film as a "dramatic story of the key role of wholesaling in the jet age of distribution", with an order for copies of the film for $125.

Although Buster plays his part as charmingly as ever and has nice interplay with sidekick Ralph Dunn, it is the weakest of the industrial films, being overburdened with a leaden treatise on the benefits of wholesaling. The critic for *Business Screen Magazine*, having conceivably watched a different film, called it "riotously funny".

The Home Owner

Directed by: Joe Parker
Produced by: John F. Long
Presented by: John F. Long
Written by: Joe Parker, Buster Keaton (uncredited)
Released: 1961
Length: 22 minutes

Cast:
Buster Keaton – Home owner
Bob Hawk – Narrator / Estate agent
John F. Long – Man in bowling alley (uncredited)

Director of photography: Leo Tover
Film editor: Basil Wrangell
Production company: Skirball Productions

Buster expresses interest in buying a John F. Long home in Maryvale, near Phoenix, Arizona. He is shown around the various homes on offer at the John F. Long International Home Show.

A promotional film for John F. Long homes. Director Joe Parker was the producer of Buster's first TV series.

Although initially successful, demographic changes in the 1970s led to under-investment in the urban village of Maryvale, with the consequent increase in poverty and crime.

The film is dialogue free, save a final "wouldn't you like to live in Maryvale too?", with otherwise only a voiceover and communication on-screen taking place by means of placards.

Having admired a display of awards won by John F. Long homes, Buster flashes the camera a glimpse of his own honorary Oscar, presented to him the previous year, which he's carrying under his jacket.

Buster's cartwheel into a neighbour's pool is particularly impressive.

The Triumph of Lester Snapwell

Directed by: James Calhoun
Produced by: Eastman Kodak
Written by: Ralph Berton
Released: 1963
Length: 22 minutes

Cast:
Buster Keaton – Lester Snapwell
Sigrid Nelsson – Clementine
Nina Varela – Mama

Production company: Eastman Kodak

> The year is 1868, and photography is in its infancy. Buster uses a cumbersome new camera to try to capture the heart of Clementine. On being accidentally killed by Clementine's mother, he is transported to 1888 by Father Time, when photography has become a little easier. Capturing Clementine still being fraught with difficulty however, he is moved on to the 1920s. A mishap with flash powder once again does for him, and he is ushered forward to 1957, and finally on to 1963 and the fool-proof Instamatic.

One of the more elaborate of Buster's industrial films. No stand-in is used for the close-ups of Buster's hand here, and his missing fingertip is all too apparent.

Although in colour, it is shot in the manner of an early silent short, which works well in both the period and contemporary scenes. The opening title card, "Our hero, Lester Snapwell, had two loves … his camera and his girl, Clementine (in that order)", is a clear nod to the opening of *The General*.

The Railrodder

Directed by: Gerald Potterton, Buster Keaton (uncredited), John Spotton
  (uncredited)
Produced by: Julian Biggs
Presented by: National Film Board of Canada
Written by: Gerald Potterton, Buster Keaton (uncredited)

Released: 2 October 1965
Length: 25 minutes

Cast:
Buster Keaton – The railrodder

Camera: Robert Humble
Editing by: Jo Kirkpatrick, Gerald Potterton
Music by: Eldon Rathburn
Sound effects: Karl du Plessis
Sound recording: George Croll, Ted Haley
Production company: National Film Board of Canada

Seeing a full-page ad in the *Sunday Times* exhorting him to "See Canada Now!", Buster jumps from Westminster Bridge and swims the Atlantic in order to do just that. Having ascertained he has arrived in Canada, and the Pacific Ocean is 3,982½ miles away, he climbs on a "speeder" open-top rail maintenance vehicle in order to take a nap. But he accidentally sets it off westwards an embarks on a coast-to-coast adventure aboard the speeder – cooking, washing, playing patience, knitting, doing his laundry, napping, taking photographs, carrying out maintenance and generally taking in the sights along the way. On arrival at the west coast, while he is enjoying the view of the Pacific, a Japanese Buster look-a-like emerges from the ocean and heads back east on Buster's speeder.

Filming began on 5 September 1964, near Halifax, Nova Scotia. Naturally, the filming was chronological, travelling from east to west, and much of the action was improvised.

The opening sequence filmed in London used a stunt double, with Buster being superimposed in post-production.

As was documented in *Buster Keaton Rides Again*, a gag where Buster unfolds a giant map while travelling over a bridge caused deep division between actor and director. Buster was adamant that the stunt wasn't dangerous and to fake it with some kind of cut or close-up would ruin the effect.

Buster Keaton Rides Again

Directed by: John Spotton
Produced by: Julian Biggs
Fondly presented by: National Film Board of Canada
Commentary by: Donald Brittain
Released: 30 October 1965
Length: 55 minutes

Cast:
Buster Keaton – Himself
Eleanor Keaton – Herself (uncredited)
Gerald Potterton – Himself (uncredited)
Michael Kane – Narrator (uncredited)

Photographed by: John Spotton
Picture editor: John Spotton
Music editor: Malca Gillson
Location sound: Barry Ferguson
Sound editor: Sidney Pearson
Re-recording by: Ron Alexander, George Croll
Production company: National Film Board of Canada

A documentary about the making of *The Railrodder*. Buster is seen discussing shots with the director, choreographing extras, playing cards and the ukulele, watching ball games on TV, and best of all, indulging in a little reminiscence. He is also seen to be decidedly ill at ease before and during a press conference.

A fascinating glimpse of Buster at work and at play – as ever, equally committed to both. His beautiful relationship with Eleanor also shines through. His occasional racking cough is a reminder that he is in worse health than he possibly realises. He was to pass away within a year.

Buster was less keen on the film, and later confided to Eleanor that he felt the public shouldn't see his private side but only the "Buster Keaton" character.

The film uses stills from Rudi Blesh's just-published biography *Keaton*.

Interestingly, while *The Railrodder* was in colour, *Buster Keaton Rides Again* is in black and white, giving it a period feel.

Film

Directed by: Alan Schneider, Samuel Beckett (uncredited)
Produced by: Barney Rosset
Written by: Samuel Beckett
Released: 8 January 1966
Premiere: 4 September 1965, Venice Film Festival
Length: 22 minutes

Cast:
Buster Keaton – "O"
Nell Harrison – Old woman
James Karen – Passer-by
Susan Reed – Passer-by

Director of photography: Boris Kaufman
Edited by: Sidney Meyers
Production company: Evergreen Theatre
Distributed by: Milestone Film and Video

We follow a figure in a heavy black overcoat, always facing away from the camera but recognisable from his porkpie hat, through the city streets back to his bare apartment. Obviously seeking isolation, he takes great pains to draw the blinds, cover a mirror, put out his cat and dog, cover his goldfish … He sits in a rocking chair and lovingly looks through old photographs before ripping them up and throwing them to the floor. The camera tracks around the room and turns to show the face of the figure for the first time, and reveal that he is staring at his own image.

Samuel Beckett's sole cinematic venture is certainly a challenge. Buster found it so, and never rated the work.

Buster was not Alan Schneider and Samuel Beckett's first choice of lead, or indeed their second choice. It was only when Jack MacGowran and Zero Mostel proved to be unavailable that Buster's name came up. And even then he may not have got the gig had Chaplin been free. Buster's name was suggested by James Karen, who plays the passer-by in the film, along with his wife Susan Reed. Apparently neither writer nor director were overly familiar with Buster's work and so Karen arranged for a number of Buster's films to be privately screened at the Museum of Modern Art over three days.

The Scribe

Directed by: John Sebert
Produced by: Ann and Kenneth Heeley-Ray
Presented by: Construction Safety Associations of Ontario
Screenplay: Paul Sutherland, Clifford Braggins
Released: 1 May 1966
Length: 30 minutes

Cast:
Buster Keaton – Journalist
Jack Creley – Newspaper editor (uncredited)
Cec Linder – O'Malley (uncredited)
Larry Reynolds – Stunt double (uncredited)

Photography: Mike Lente
Film and sound editor: Kenneth Heeley-Ray
Music by: Quartet Productions Limited
Production company: Construction Safety Associations of Ontario, Film-Tele
  Productions
Executive Producers: Raymond Walters, James Collier

> Cub reporter Buster is sent to a building site to report on safety aspects after a string of stories of accidents in the city. His well-meaning attempts to remind the construction workers of the "Take 16 Steps and Live" safety tips are not always successfully put across, and he is pursued by an increasing number of irate workmen.

Eleanor Keaton's *Buster Keaton Remembered* lists the release as 8 January 1966. The working title, seen on slates in production stills, was *The Reporter*.

Buster's last appearance on film was shot in Toronto in October 1965. The director remembered that Buster was still smoking three or four packs of cigarettes a day and would go into coughing fits lasting several minutes. Nevertheless, even at 70 years old, he tackles the exacting role with vigour, clearly the last thing on his mind being to go gentle into that good night.

On the flight home, oxygen had to be administered to him, and on arrival he was taken to his doctor. X-rays revealed he had inoperable lung cancer and was given up to three months to live, although Buster was not told of the diagnosis. His final job was to take part in a sketch with Lucille Ball as part of a televised tribute to Stan Laurel, who had died on 23 February 1965.

OTHER ON-SCREEN APPEARANCES

The Round-Up (1920, Paramount) (uncredited)

Directed by George Melford, with Roscoe "Fatty" Arbuckle, Mabel Julienne Scott, Irving Cummings

Roscoe needed an American Indian to die in spectacular fashion. Step forward Buster. (Some sources mistake this film for *The Iron Mule* (1925, Educational Pictures) which was directed by Roscoe (as William B. Goodrich), and starred Al St. John. There is no sign of Buster in this short – the Keaton connection is that the iron mule in question is the locomotive from *Our Hospitality*.)

Seeing Stars (1922, First National)

With Charles Chaplin, Jackie Coogan, Constance and Norma Talmadge

This promotional film was shot at a special dinner at the Ambassador Hotel, Los Angeles. Buster (playing the waiter) and Chaplin appear together on screen for the first time.

Character Studies (c. 1925)

With Carter DeHaven, Roscoe "Fatty" Arbuckle, Rudolph Valentino

Magician DeHaven impersonates a series of stars who, through the magic of film, appear as themselves.

Brotherly Love (1928, MGM) (uncredited, unconfirmed)

Directed by Charles Reisner, with Karl Dane, George K. Arthur, Jean Arthur

This film is probably lost – a set of sound discs is in the UCLA film library, but no copy of the film itself is known to exist – and so it's hard to know whether Buster appears. A production still shows him with razor in hand alongside Karl Dane. But whether Buster just happened to be on the set, or the scene, if it was shot, even made the film, we can't be sure. His participation is unlikely, however, as there is no mention of Buster in reviews and listings at the time.

The Baby Cyclone (1928, MGM) (uncredited)

Directed by A. Edward Sutherland, with Lew Cody, Aileen Pringle

Lew Cody was required to fall down a flight of stairs, but neither Cody nor the stuntmen could make it suitably funny. Buster, filming *The Cameraman* on the same lot, was tasked with stunt. The fall was so realistic that when he saw it, Louis B. Mayer hauled Buster into his office and forbade him from any further such recklessness. Nevertheless Buster received a check for $7.50 for his trouble. The uncashed check, now framed, was hanging on the wall of his den when Kevin Brownlow visited him there in 1964.

Tide of Empire (1929, MGM)

Directed by Allan Dwan, with Renée Adorée, Tom Keene

Buster has a cameo as a drunk thrown out of a bar.

Voice of Hollywood (1929, Wardour Films)

With Robert Woolsey, Cliff Edwards

A series of cameos playing out brief skits in front of a lion's cage.

The Hollywood Revue of 1929 (1929, MGM)

Directed by Charles Reisner, with Conrad Nagel, Jack Benny, Joan Crawford, John Gilbert, Norma Shearer

A musical revue featuring the MGM roster of stars, with Buster as Princess Rajah performing The Dance of the Sea.

The March of Time (1930, MGM, unreleased)

Directed by Charles Reisner, with Bing Crosby, Ramon Novarro, William Collier Sr., William Collier Jr.

Intended as a follow up to *The Hollywood Revue of 1929*, MGM shelved it as they thought, bizarrely, that interest in musicals had peaked. A German version, *Wir Schalten um auf Hollywood!*, did get a release. Buster plays a caveman in the film, pretty much the only cast member not to be playing themselves.

The Stolen Jools (1931, Paramount)

Directed by William C. McGann, with Wallace Beery, Laurel and Hardy, Maurice Chevalier

Another all-star extravaganza with Edward G. Robinson, Joan Crawford, Gary Cooper, Douglas Fairbanks Jr., Loretta Young, and Bebe Daniels and Ben Lyon, in which Buster plays a policeman.

Hollywood on Parade A-6 (1932, Louis Lewyn Productions)

Directed by Louis Lewyn, with Lew Cody

Buster appears in at least one of the *Hollywood on Parade* series of shorts – here featuring his own so-called "land yacht", which was his temporary home at the time. Lew Cody plays his second-in-command.

La Fiesta de Santa Barbara (1935, MGM)

Directed by Louis Lewyn, with Ida Lupino, Harpo Marx, Gary Cooper

Yet another all-star revue, this time with a Mexican theme. Thirteen-year-old Judy Garland appears as one of The Garland Sisters. Buster referees a bullfight. "Best comedy moments are provided by Buster Keaton" – *Variety*.

Hollywood Cavalcade (1939, Twentieth Century-Fox)

Directed by Irving Cummings, Buster's segment directed by Mal St. Clair (uncredited), with Alice Faye, Don Ameche, J. Edward Bromberg

Set in the pioneering days of Hollywood, Buster plays himself in a silent film-within-a-film, and receives thanks in the credits. Also appearing as themselves are Mack Sennett and Al Jolson.

Ol' Strike Thrower

Hollywood, July 11.
Alice Faye stood up manfully under a barrage of custard pies in 'Hollywood Cavalcade' at 20th-Fox until Buster Keaton was called to the pitching mound. Whereupon she called for a stand-in.
'Keaton's a professional,' she said.

New Moon (1940, MGM) (uncredited)

Directed by Robert Z. Leonard, with Nelson Eddy, Jeanette MacDonald, May Boland

Buster had an entire sub-plot as a prisoner in the film, but this was completely cut for release (reportedly because he stole the film from its stars) leaving him as just an uncredited extra, occasionally seen in the background.

The Villain Still Pursued Her (1940, RKO)

Directed by Edward F. Cline, with Hugh Herbert, Anita Louise, Alan Mowbray

Reunited with Eddie Cline, Buster plays William Dalton, ultimately a force for good in this deliberately and delightfully over-the-top period melodrama, and again is given a custard pie to brandish.

Li'l Abner (1940, RKO)

Directed by Albert S. Rogell, with Jeff York, Martha O'Driscoll, Mona Ray, Johnnie Morris

Buster appears as Lonesome Polecat in this best-forgotten mess of a film. At least he gets to work with Al St. John for one last time, and with his sister Louise.

Forever and a Day (1943, RKO)

Buster's segment directed by Victor Saville, with Cedric Hardwicke, Jessie Matthews, Charles Laughton

The film is a series of vignettes featuring a stellar cast of hundreds of mainly British stars including Ray Milland, Claude Rains, Ida Lupino, Merle Oberon and Elsa Lanchester. The film boasts seven directors and some 22 writers. Buster plays a plumber's assistant who demonstrates the ingenious features of a newly installed shower.

San Diego, I Love You (1944, Universal)

Directed by Reginald Le Borg, with Jon Hall, Louise Allbritton, Edward Everett Horton

Buster crops up as a rather cantankerous bus driver who is goaded into taking a detour along the beach.

That's the Spirit (1945, Universal)

Directed by Charles Lamont, with Jack Oakie, Peggy Ryan, June Vincent

Buster plays L.M., a manager in the complaints department in heaven.

That Night with You (1945, Universal)

Directed by William A. Seiter, with Franchot Tone, Susanna Foster, David Bruce

Buster plays Sam, a short-order cook in an all-night diner.

She Went to the Races (1945, MGM) (uncredited)

Directed by Willis Goldbeck, with James Craig, Frances Gifford, Ava Gardner

Buster's main contribution to the film was a gag writer, but he does have a minuscule part as a bellboy.

God's Country (1946, Action Pictures)

Directed by Robert E. Tansey, with Robert Lowery, Helen Gilbert, William Farnum

Dressed in buckskins and a Davy Crockett hat, Buster plays Old Tarp, a.k.a. Mr. Boone.

El Colmillo de Buda (1949, Dyana, Oro Films, Mexico)

Directed by Juan Bustillo Oro, with Amalia Aguilar, Rafael Alcayde, Armando Arriola

Buster has a bit part in this yarn about the theft of the tooth of the Buddha.

The Lovable Cheat (1949, Skyline Pictures)

Directed by Richard Oswald, with Charles Ruggles, Peggy Ann Garner, Richard Ney

Buster is Goulard, a creditor of Charles Ruggles' con artist.

You're My Everything (1949, Twentieth Century-Fox)

Directed by Walter Lang, with Dan Dailey, Anne Baxter, Anne Revere

Buster plays a butler in another silent film-within-a-film segment. Anne Baxter accidentally spills a drink on him, and, outraged, he pulls out his trademark porkpie hat and storms off.

In the Good Old Summertime (1949, MGM)

Directed by Robert Z. Leonard, with Judy Garland, Van Johnson, S.Z. Sakall

Back with MGM for his first credited role in nearly ten years, Buster plays Hickey, working in his uncle's music shop. Buster also wrote and directed the scene where Judy Garland and Van Johnson first meet.

Sunset Boulevard (1950, Paramount)

Directed by Billy Wilder, with William Holden, Gloria Swanson, Erich von Stroheim

Finally appearing once again in a top-flight Hollywood film, Buster plays himself as one of three "waxworks" – with Anna Q. Nillson and H.B. Warner – who convene to play bridge with fading silent star Norma Desmond, played magnificently by Gloria Swanson.

Limelight (1952, United Artists)

Directed by Charles Chaplin, with Charles Chaplin, Claire Bloom, Nigel Bruce

Together on screen at last (although they had both appeared in the 1922 one-reel *Seeing Stars*) Buster plays the part of Chaplin's sidekick, Calvero.

L'Incantevole Nemica (1953, Orso Films, Italy)

Directed by Claudio Gora, with Silvana Pampanini, Robert Lamoureux

Buster is seen in a comedy sketch that was filmed in a theatre in Milan where he was appearing with his wife Eleanor. The film was not released in the US.

Around the World in 80 Days (1956, United Artists)

Directed by Michael Anderson, with David Niven, Cantinflas, Shirley MacLaine

In an all-star cast once again, alongside the likes of Marlene Dietrich, Ronald Colman, John Gielgud, George Raft, Peter Lorre and Frank Sinatra, Buster plays the conductor on the train from San Francisco to Fort Kearney.

The Adventures of Huckleberry Finn (1960, MGM)

Directed by Michael Curtiz, with Tony Randall, Archie Moore, Eddie Hodges

In a spurious travelling circus segment, Buster plays an ageing lion tamer.

It's a Mad, Mad, Mad, Mad World (1963, United Artists)

Directed by Stanley Kramer, with Spencer Tracy, Milton Berle, Sid Caesar

In a cast of hundreds, Buster appears alongside Ethel Merman, Mickey Rooney, Jimmy Durante, The Three Stooges – and Roscoe Arbuckle's first wife Minta Durfee. Buster's performance fell victim to the need to cut the film back from its original 192 minutes, his role as Jimmy the Crook being largely eliminated.

Pajama Party (1964, American International)

Directed by Don Weis, with Tommy Kirk, Annette Funicello, Elsa Lanchester

The first of Buster's American International Pictures "Beach Party" movies, which was the fourth in the series, playing Chief Rotten Eagle. Buster had begun filming a musical comedy in 1962, *Ten Girls Ago*, with teen idol Dion, but the film was not completed.

Beach Blanket Bingo (1965, American International)

Directed by William Asher, with Frankie Avalon, Annette Funicello, Deborah Walley

Buster plays a character called Buster, dressed in his familiar Keaton outfit.

How to Stuff a Wild Bikini (1965, American International)

Directed by William Asher, with Annette Funicello, Dwayne Hickman, Brian Donlevy

Here Buster takes on the role of Bwana, a witch doctor with a penchant for love potions.

Sergeant Deadhead (1965, American International)

Directed by Norman Taurog, with Frankie Avalon, Deborah Walley, Cesar Romero

As Airman Blinken, Buster is hardly present in his fourth and final Beach Party movie.

War Italian Style (1965, American International)

Directed by Luigi Scattini, with Franco Franchi, Ciccio Ingrassia

As the film wasn't released outside Italy until 1967, this is effectively Buster's last on-screen appearance in his home country. Unlikely as it sounds, Buster plays the Nazi General von Kassler. The final shot is particularly apt – as a mark of the character's inherent decency, his captors hand him civilian clothes and let him go. He utters his one line of dialogue, "Thank you", and, appearing in the full Keaton outfit – porkpie hat, baggy suit with half-tied bow tie, and slap shoes – he turns to look towards the camera before heading off into the Italian countryside.

A Funny Thing Happened on the Way to the Forum (1966, United Artists)

Directed by Richard Lester, with Zero Mostel, Phil Silvers, Michael Crawford

In his final feature-length film, Buster is Erronius "a befuddled old man". Buster was clearly ill during filming and a double was needed for some, though certainly not all, of the more energetic scenes.

Directed by Buster Keaton

In the year between finishing the Educational Pictures shorts and embarking on the Columbia shorts, Buster was contracted with MGM as a gag man and general consultant. In this time he directed three one-reel films, known as "miniatures".

Life in Sometown, USA (1938, MGM)

With Carey Wilson, William Bailey, Margaret Bert

A look at some antiquated laws that are still on the statute books.

Hollywood Handicap (1938, MGM)

With the Original Sing Band, Mickey Rooney, Al Jolson, Ruby Keeler, Bing Crosby

A group of stable boys raise money to run their horse at the Hollywood Derby at Santa Anita, which is attended by more stars than there are in heaven.

Streamlined Swing (1938, MGM)

With the Original Sing Band, Richard Cramer, Lester Dorr

A group of railway waiters set up a carriage as a diner on Wilshire Boulevard, Los Angeles. The script was co-written by Marion Mack.

Key Television Appearances

As well as appearing in probably over a hundred commercials – for Colgate toothpaste in 1956 through to Pepsi-Cola in 1965 – Buster took part in several notable television programmes. He fully embraced the new medium from relatively early on, much to the bemusement of his many of contemporaries including Chaplin and Lloyd. The most significant of the dozens of shows and series that he took part in are listed here.

The Ed Wynn Show (1949)

One of Buster's first TV appearances was on 9 December 1949, recreating the can of molasses scene from *The Butcher Boy* with Ed Wynn.

The Buster Keaton Show (1949–50)

A series of some sixteen 30-minute comedies, premiering on Thursday 22 December 1949 (incidentally taking over *The Ed Wynn Show* slot, which moved to Saturdays). They were produced by Joe Parker, directed by Philippe DeLacy

and written by Clyde Bruckman and Henry Taylor. Filmed in front of a live audience, the shows were initially aired only locally on KTTV Hollywood.

The series was critically well received. *Daily Variety* wrote of the first show, "An old timer came into his own last night over a new medium and it looks like television has a new 'must see' program that is very likely to become a permanent fixture. … Keaton has lost none of his touch with the passing years."

The Buster Keaton Show (1951)

Premiering on 9 May 1951, and nationally syndicated by Consolidated Television as *Life with Buster Keaton* in 1952, thirteen 30-minute episodes were made. This time filming was without a live audience, which made it less enjoyable for Buster. The shows were produced by Carl K. Hittleman, writers included Clyde Bruckman, Harold Goodwin and Jay Sommers and directors Arthur Hilton and Eddie Cline.

The individual episodes were entitled "The Army Story", "The Bakery Story", "The Collapsible Clerk", "The Detective Story", "The Fishing Story", "The Gymnasium Story", "The Haunted House", "The Little Theatre", "The Shakespeare Story", "The Time Machine", "The Western Story" and "The Gorilla Story".

Some episodes were combined and released in the UK in 1953 by British Lion Films as *The Misadventures of Buster Keaton*.

Douglas Fairbanks Jr. Presents (1954)

This was a series of 30-minute dramas produced by NBC. On 14 July 1954, Buster starred in "The Awakening", based on Gogol's "The Overcoat". It is reported to be Buster's first completely dramatic role.

Best of Broadway (1954)

An hour-long anthology from CBS, Buster appeared in "The Man who Came to Dinner" alongside Monty Woolley, Joan Bennett, Bert Lahr and Merle Oberon. The show was broadcast on 13 October 1954.

Screen Directors Playhouse (1955)

Buster starred in an episode entitled "The Silent Partner" on 21 December 1955. It was produced by Hal Roach Studios.

Circus Time (1956)

Buster features with Eleanor in a segment from this ABC variety series.

The Martha Raye Show (1956)

Buster and Martha Raye

This appearance is particularly interesting as Buster recreates the concert scene from *Limelight*, with Martha Raye taking on Chaplin's part. Marhta Raye herself had appeared with Chaplin in *Monsieur Verdoux* in 1947. There had been rumours, later confirmed by Claire Bloom among others, that Chaplin had felt that he was being upstaged by Buster during rehearsals for *Limelight* to the extent that, irritated by Buster's ingenuity, he had cut down Buster's part in the final film. Chaplin's assistant Jerry Epstein refuted this.

What is interesting is that this sketch with Raye has much more business from Buster, who for his part is actually much funnier than in the original. Whether this inventive extra material is what had annoyed Chaplin in rehearsals, or what may have been cut from the released version of *Limelight*, or indeed had been dreamt up by Buster specifically for the television show, we may never know.

Producer's Showcase (1956)

An anthology of 90-minute programmes for NBC, Buster starred in the musical "The Lord Don't Play Favorites" with Robert Stack, Kay Starr and Louis Armstrong. The programme aired on 17 September 1956.

This Is Your Life (1957)

Ralph Edwards surprised Buster with the big red book (in black and white of course) on 3 April 1957. As well as Eleanor, his sons, and brother Harry and sister Louise, guests included Red Skelton, Eddie Cline and, plugging the forthcoming *The Buster Keaton Story*, Donald O'Connor.

The Adventures of Mr. Pastry (1958)

This was a pilot for ITV in the UK, filmed in 1955 but was not taken up. It was eventually broadcast on 21 June 1958. Buster appeared alongside Richard Hearne as Mr. Pastry and Peggy Mount as the landlady. While Buster was filming in England, his mother Myra died on 21 July after a long illness.

Playhouse 90 (1958)

Another NBC 90-minute anthology, Buster starred in "The Innocent Sleep" on 5 June 1958.

Sunday Showcase (1960)

Buster starred alongside Christopher Plummer in "After Hours" on 7 February.

Candid Camera (1961)

Buster appeared at the counter of a diner, dropping his watch and toupee in his soup and leaning over and accidentally ripping the sleeve off his jacket.

Twilight Zone (1961)

The groundbreaking 30-minute anthology from CBS hosted by Rod Serling. Buster starred in "Once Upon a Time", directed by Norman Z. McLeod and broadcast on 15 December 1961.

The Scene Stealers (1962)

An hour-long March of Dimes musical comedy sketch show on CBS with Ed Wynn, Rosemary Clooney, Jimmy Durante, Eartha Kitt and Jack Lemmon. It reportedly first aired in either January or April 1962, but was possibly syndicated to local markets.

Route 66 (1962)

A series of 60-minute adventures produced by CBS, Buster appeared in "Journey to Nineveh" on 28 September 1962.

The Greatest Show on Earth (1964)

A series of hour-long dramas from ABC. Buster appeared in "You're Alright, Ivy" on 28 April 1964. It was directed by and starred Jack Palance, with Joe E. Brown and Joan Blondell.

A Salute to Stan Laurel (1965)

Buster's last screen appearance was in this 60-minute tribute in a sketch with Lucille Ball, which was broadcast on 23 November 1965.

1895	**4 October,** Joseph Keaton born
1897	named "Buster"
1899	performs with his parents at a children's matinee; **April,** has end of right index finger amputated after a wrangle with a clothes mangle
1900	**April,** stands in for his injured father in The Two Keatons **October,** officially joins the family act and The Two Keatons become The Three Keatons
1901	**11 March,** makes his New York debut
1902	**October,** starts school in the morning and leaves in the afternoon, never to return
1904	**25 August,** brother Harry ("Jingles") born
1906	plays in *Little Lord Fauntleroy* and *East Lynne* with the Fenberg Stock Company throughout New England; **30 October,** sister Louise born
1907	**1 December,** The Three Keatons barred from New York City for two years for breach of the child labour laws
1909	**1 July,** The Three Keatons set off for London, returning after just a week of performing at the Palace Theatre; **July,** *Ben's Kid,* Roscoe Arbuckle's first single-reel film, is released; **October,** press ads announce The Three Keatons' return to the New York stage now that Buster is 16 and outside the jurisdiction of the NY Society for the Prevention of Cruelty to Children. Buster has of course just turned 14
1910	**February,** Buster (reportedly) sustains concussion and Joe loses three teeth in a rail accident in Harrisburg, Pennsylvania
1912	**4 July,** Keystone Pictures Studio formed by Mack Sennett
1913	Arbuckle joins Sennett as a Keystone Kop; William Randolph Hearst suggests the Keatons appear in a film series based on the comic strip *Bringing Up Father* – Joe vetoes the idea

1914	Chaplin joins Keystone, on $150 a week	
		Films released:
1917	**March,** meets Arbuckle	*The Butcher Boy; The Rough House; His Wedding Night; Oh Doctor!; Coney Island; A Country Hero*
1918	**July,** enlists in the army; **August,** sent to France to work as a cryptographer and entertainer	*Out West; The Bell Boy; Moonshine; Good Night, Nurse!; The Cook*
1919	**March,** returns to the US; **23 December,** signs with Joe Schenck to make two-reeler comedies	*Back Stage; The Hayseed*
1920	**January,** "Buster" Keaton Studios open for business	*The Garage; One Week; The Saphead; The Round-Up; Convict 13; The Scarecrow; Neighbors*
1921	**31 May,** marries Natalie Talmadge; **17 September,** Roscoe Arbuckle arrested for manslaughter	*The Haunted House; Hard Luck; The "High Sign"; The Goat; The Playhouse; The Boat*
1922	**12 April,** Arbuckle acquitted after third trial; **2 June,** Joseph Talmadge Keaton born, later to be called by Natalie's preferred name of Jimmy	*The Paleface; Seeing Stars; Cops; My Wife's Relations; The Blacksmith; The Frozen North; The Electric House; Day Dreams*
1923	**13 January,** signs with Metro to make feature-length films	*The Balloonatic; The Love Nest; Three Ages; Our Hospitality*
1924	**3 February,** Robert Talmadge Keaton born	*Sherlock Jr.; The Navigator*
1925	**11 February,** Jean Havez dies	*Seven Chances; Go West*
1926	builds Italian villa; **20 October,** almost half of the 112 pages of *Variety* are dedicated to congratulating Joe Schenck on ten years in the business, including an article by Buster	*Battling Butler; The General*

1927		*College*
1928	**26 January,** signs with MGM*	*Steamboat Bill, Jr.; The Baby Cyclone; The Cameraman*
1929		*Tide of Empire; Spite Marriage; The Hollywood Revue of 1929*
1930	**March,** Buster's voice is heard onscreen for the first time	*Free and Easy; Estrellados; Doughboys; The March of Time; ¡De Frente, Marchen!*
1931	fire causes $10,000 damage to the Italian villa	*Parlor, Bedroom and Bath; The Stolen Jools; Sidewalks of New York; Casanova wider Willen; Buster se Marie*
1932	**25 July,** Natalie files for divorce; **5 October,** signs contract with MGM relinquishing top billing	*The Passionate Plumber; Le Plombier Amoureux*
1933	**8 January,** marries Mae Scriven; **2 February,** Louis B. Mayer terminates Buster's contract with MGM; **29 June,** Roscoe Arbuckle dies; **21 October,** having discovered his divorce from Natalie had not been finalised until August, marries Mae Scriven again	*What! No Beer?; Hollywood on Parade No. A-6*
1934	Natalie changes Jimmy and Bobby's names from Keaton to Talmadge	*The Gold Ghost; Allez Oop!; Le Roi des Champs-Élysées*
1935		*Palooka from Paducah; One Run Elmer; Hayseed Romance; Tars and Stripes; The E-Flat Man; The Timid Young Man; La Fiesta de Santa Barbara*
1936	**14 October,** divorce from Mae becomes absolute	*The Invader; Three on a Limb; Grand Slam Opera; Blue Blazes; The Chemist; Mixed Magic*

1937	**July,** contracted as gag man and consultant for MGM	*Jail Bait*; *Ditto*; *Love Nest on Wheels*
1938	Jingles introduces Buster to 18-year-old MGM dancer Eleanor Norris	*Life in Sometown, USA*; *Hollywood Handicap*; *Streamlined Swing (all as director)*
1939		*Pest from the West*; *Mooching Through Georgia*; *Hollywood Cavalcade*;
1940	**29 May,** marries Eleanor Norris	*Nothing But Pleasure*; *Pardon My Berth Marks*; *The Taming of the Snood*; *New Moon*; *The Spook Speaks*; *The Villain Still Pursued Her*; *Li'l Abner*; *His Ex Marks the Spot*
1941	**8 July,** opens summer-stock tour in *The Gorilla*	*So You Won't Squawk?*; *General Nuisance*; *She's Oil Mine*
1942	**May,** Jimmy and Bobby have their names officially changed to Talmadge	
1943		*Forever and a Day*
1944	**December,** Buster Keaton Productions is dissolved	*San Diego, I Love You*
1945		*That's the Spirit*; *That Night with You*; *She Went to the Races*
1946	**13 January,** Joe Keaton dies **25 April,** *Lambs Will Gamble*, based on Buster's 1937 play *Marooned in Mojave*, opens; it closes 2½ weeks later	*God's Country*; *El Moderno Barba Azul*
1947	**September,** first appearance at the Cirque Médrano, Paris	
1948	sues Warner Bros for plagiarising his own life story in *April Showers*	*Un Duel à Mort*
1949	appears in summer-stock *Three Men on a Horse*;	*El Colmillo de Buda*; *The Lovable Cheat*; *You're My Everything*;

1949	5 **September,** "Comedy's Greatest Era" article by James Agee in *Life* magazine; 8 **December,** appears on *The Ed Wynn Show*; 22 **December,** first episode of *The Buster Keaton Show* airs on Los Angeles-based KTTV	*In the Good Old Summertime*
1950	*The Buster Keaton Show* (syndicated as *Life with Buster Keaton* in 1952) airs nationally; 12 **December,** "Santa Claus for Hire" sketch on Ed Sullivan's *Toast of the Town***	*Sunset Boulevard*; *The Misadventures of Buster Keaton*
1951	9 **May,** the second season of *The Buster Keaton Show* airs 22 **December,** starts filming *Limelight* with Charlie Chaplin	
1952	**May,** *Harper's Bazaar* run "Last Call for a Clown", an appreciation of Buster by critic Walter Kerr; 27 **September,** begins second three-week run at the Cirque Médrano, Paris, following a two-week stint in Toronto, Canada	*Limelight*
1953		*L'Incantevole Nemica*
1954	Raymond Rohauer starts to collect and preserve Buster's films; 8 **January – 4 February,** final appearances at the Cirque Médrano, Paris; 14 **July,** appears in NBC's *Douglas Fairbanks Jr. Presents* episode "The Awakening"	
1955	21 **July,** Myra Keaton dies	
1956	**June,** Buster and Eleanor move into their ranch house in the San Fernando Valley	*Around the World in 80 Days*

1957	appears in summer-stock *Merton of the Movies*; acts as technical advisor for *The Buster Keaton Story*; **3 April,** "This Is Your Life"	
1958	tours in revival of *Three Men on a Horse*	
1960	appears with Eleanor in a seven-month tour of the musical *Once Upon a Mattress*; **January,** *My Wonderful World of Slapstick* is published; **4 April,** presented with honorary Oscar	*The Adventures of Huckleberry Finn*
1961	**22 October,** Joe Schenck dies	
1962	**6 February,** Raymond Rohauer organises a 20-city tour of Germany with *The General*; **December,** Cinémathèque française honours Buster with a special retrospective	*Ten Girls Ago*
1963	**21 January,** Al St. John dies	*It's a Mad, Mad, Mad, Mad World*
1964		*Pajama Party*
1965	**23 November,** final TV appearance in "A Salute to Stan Laurel" with Lucille Ball	*Beach Blanket Bingo*; *The Railrodder*; *Buster Keaton Rides Again*; *How to Stuff a Wild Bikini*; *Sergeant Deadhead*; *Film*; *War Italian Style*
1966	**1 February,** dies aged 70	*The Scribe*; *A Funny Thing Happened on the Way to the Forum*

* Despite the existence of a facsimile of the contract showing this date, *Motion Picture News*, *Exhibitors Herald* and other contemporary journals reported that Buster had already signed by December 1927. See *The Cameraman* (p. 105).

** Other sources, including Eleanor Keaton's celebratory *Buster Keaton Remembered*, give 5 November.

Bibliography

Books

Anobile, Richard J. (ed.), *Buster Keaton's The General* (Avon, 1975)

Bengtson, John, *Silent Echoes: Discovering Early Hollywood Through the Films of Buster Keaton* (Santa Monica Press, 1999)

Blesh, Rudi, *Keaton* (Macmillan, 1966)

Brownlow, Kevin, *The Parade's Gone By …* (Bonanza Books, New York, 1968)

Brownlow, Kevin and John Kobal, *Hollywood: The Pioneers* (Alfred A. Knopf, 1979)

Cottage Grove Historical Society, *The Day Buster Smiled: The 1926 Filming of "The General" by Buster Keaton* (Eugene Print, 1998)

Curtis, James, *Buster Keaton: A Filmmaker's Life* (Alfred A. Knopf, 2022)

Foote, Lisle, *Buster Keaton's Crew: The Team Behind His Silent Films* (McFarland, 2014)

Gehring, Wes D., *Buster Keaton in His Own Time: What the Responses of 1920s Critics Reveal* (McFarland, 2018)

Horton, Andrew (ed.), *Buster Keaton's Sherlock Jr.* (Cambridge University Press, 1997)

Keaton, Buster and Charles Samuels, *My Wonderful World of Slapstick* (1960, republ. Da Capo Press, 1988)

Keaton, Eleanor and Jeffrey Vance, *Buster Keaton Remembered* (Harry N. Abrams, 2001)

Kerr, Walter, *The Silent Clowns* (Knopf, 1975)

Kline, Jim, *The Complete Films of Buster Keaton* (Citadel Press, 1993)

Knopf, Robert, *The Theater and Cinema of Buster Keaton* (Princeton University Press, 1999)

McPherson, Edward, *Tempest in a Flat Hat* (Faber and Faber, 2004)

Meade, Marion, *Buster Keaton: Cut to the Chase* (Harper Collins, 1995)

Merton, Paul, *Silent Comedy* (Random House, 2007)

Moews, Daniel, *Buster Keaton: The Silent Features Close Up* (University of California Press, 1977)

Neibaur, James L., *Arbuckle and Keaton: Their 14 Film Collaborations* (McFarland, 2007)

Neibaur, James L., *The Fall of Buster Keaton: His Films for MGM, Educational Pictures, and Columbia* (Scarecrow Press, 2010)

Oldham, Gabriella, *Keaton's Silent Shorts: Beyond the Laughter* (Southern Illinois University Press, 1999)

Robinson, David, *Buster Keaton* (Secker & Warburg, 1969)

Neil Sinyard, *Silent Movies* (1990, Smithmark)

Smith, Imogen Sara, *Buster Keaton: The Persistence of Comedy* (Gambit, 2008)

Stevens, Dana, *Camera Man: Buster Keaton, the Dawn of Cinema, and the Invention of the Twentieth Century* (Atria Books, 2022)

Sweeney, Kevin W. (ed.), *Buster Keaton Interviews* (University Press of Mississippi, 2007)

Wead, George and George Lellis, *The Film Career of Buster Keaton* (Redgrave, 1977)

Yallop, David, *The Day the Laughter Stopped* (Constable, 2014)

Periodicals

Camera!

Exhibitors Herald

Exhibitors Trade Review

Film Bulletin

Film Comment

The Film Daily

Film Quarterly

Filmplay

Films in Review

Hollywood

Life

Los Angeles Evening Herald

Los Angeles Times

Massachusetts Review

Motion Picture Daily

Motion Picture Director of Hollywood

Motion Picture Herald

Motion Picture Magazine

Motion Picture News

Motion Picture Studio Directory and Trade Annual

Movie Weekly

Moving Picture Age

Moving Picture Weekly

Moving Picture World

New York Clipper

New York Times

Pantomime

Photoplay

The Picturegoer

Picture-Play

Pictures and Picturegoer

Screenland

Sight and Sound

Variety

Wid's Daily

Articles

Agee, James, "Comedy's Greatest Era", *Life*, 5 September 1949

Anger, Lou, "The Development of New Comedy Stars", *The Film Daily*, 3 June 1923

Arbuckle, Roscoe, "The Cost of a Laugh", *Motion Picture Magazine*, March 1918

Bishop, Christopher, "The Great Stone Face", *Film Quarterly*, Autumn 1958

Brownlow, Kevin, "Buster Keaton: The D.W. Griffith of Comedy", in John Boorman and Walter Donohoe (eds.), *Projections 4½* (Faber and Faber, 1995)

Eliot Tobias, Patricia, "A Letter from the Keaton Chronicle", *Film Quarterly*, Winter 1995–96

Everson, William, "Rediscovery: Le Roi des Champs Elysées", *Films in Review*, December 1976

Friedman, Arthur B. and Buster Keaton, "Buster Keaton: An Interview", *Film Quarterly*, Summer 1966

Garcia Lorca, Federico, "Buster Keaton Takes a Walk", *Sight and Sound*, Winter 1965

Gillett, John and James Blue, "Keaton at Venice", *Sight and Sound*, Winter 1965

Hogue, Peter, "Eye of the Storm: Buster Keaton", *Film Comment*, September/October 1995

Houston, Penelope, "The Great Blank Page", *Sight and Sound*, Spring 1968

Keaton, Buster, "What Are the Six Ages of Comedy," *The Truth about the Movies*, 1924.

Keaton, Joe, "London: Mr. Butt and Co.", *Variety*, 11 December 1909

Keaton, Joe, "The Cyclone Baby" *Photoplay*, May 1927

Keegan, J. Redmond, "Doubling Charlie Chaplin", *Pantomime*, 27 May 1922

Kingsley, Grace, "Buster Keaton's Tumbling to Success", *Movie Weekly*, 6 May 1922

Ludlam, Helen, "Yo Ho Ho – and a Buster Keaton Location", *Screenland*, March 1929

Oettinger, Malcolm H., "Tumbling to Fame", *Picture-Play*, December 1920

Oettinger, Malcolm H., "Low Comedy as a High Art", *Picture-Play*, March 1923

Reed, Rex, "Keaton: Still Making the Scene", *New York Times*, 17 October 1965

Reid, Margaret, "The Child Who Was 'Abused'", *Picture-Play*, February 1928

Robinson, David, "Rediscovery: Buster", *Sight and Sound*, Winter 1959

Russell, Spencer, "Hard Knocks Make a Man", *Filmplay*, July 1922

Squier, Emma-Lindsay, "He Really Can Smile", *Picture-Play*, July 1921

Weddle, David, "Buster Keaton", *Sight and Sound*, April 2000

"The Mournful Mirthmaker", *Pictures and Picturegoer*, October 1922

Websites

www.busterkeaton.org

www.catalog.afi.com/Person/25179-Buster-Keaton

www.imdb.com

www.archive.org

www.mediahistoryproject.org

www.silentera.com/people/actors/Keaton-Buster.html

www.sensesofcinema.com/2002/great-directors/keaton/

www.filmreference.com/Actors-and-Actresses-Hu-Ke/Keaton-Buster.html

www.whatwouldbusterkeatondo.com

Other references

A Hard Act to Follow, three-part documentary, written and produced by Kevin Brownlow and David Gill, Thames Television, 1987

Industrial Strength Keaton, two-DVD set of archival material, promotional films, television appearances and industrial films, Laughsmith Entertainment, 2005

Keaton Plus, DVD including interactive tour of locations based on *Silent Echoes* by John Bengtson, Kino, 2001

M

S

Buster with his dream team (from left)
Joe Mitchell, Clyde Bruckman, Jean Havez and Eddie Cline.